Berlin

Footprint

Neil Taylor and Nina Hamilton

G000151419

Contents

Listings

About the authors

Neil Taylor has taken advantage of a career in the travel business to visit Berlin most years since 1970. As his family left Berlin in 1933 and several members returned after the war, he has always regarded it as his second home. When there, he is often to be found ransacking the stalls of second-hand booksellers beside the Spree River for yet more old guidebooks and political biographies. He has previously written guidebooks on Estonia and the Baltic capitals and is probably the most frequent British visitor to the former Prussian capital of Königsberg, now Kaliningrad.

Nina Hamilton studied German and History at Kings College, London. She spent a year living and studying in Berlin, spending most of her time in the bars and cafés written about in this book, discussing the merits of Schopenhauer over Nietzsche and *Cookies* over *Icon*. Nina loved helping with the guidebook because it reminded her of the exciting time she had in the city. (She also plans to put her name to more publications!)

Acknowledgements

I demanded considerably more tolerance and guidance from Claire and Rachel than an author really should need. I am very grateful for their continued patience and for their faith in Berlin as a destination that definitely needs a *Footprint*.

Nina would like to thank Neil Taylor for giving her this fantastic opportunity. Her thanks also go to Helen Holtom without whom there would be no art and cinema entries, Lars Versopohl for his unparalleled film expertise and Alexander Hagelüken for his account of Berlin politics.

Thanks to Footprint author and Berlin photographer, Julius Honnor, for the accommodation section.

Introducing Berlin

Berlin has grown up fast. Capital of a reunited Germany only since 1999, it has already earned its international spurs and no longer has to settle for being simply German. Visitors can leave Berlin without having experienced Germany: American musicals, Babylonian mosaics, French bakeries and Norman Foster creations are comfortably integrated into the buildings of Schinkel and the operas of Wagner. The city that needed a long period in rehab for some serious occupation therapy is now confident enough to woo British architects, Italian designers and Polish restorers to join the burgeoining multinational community. But though reunified Berlin has undergone a level of transformation rivalled only by post-Mao Tse Tung Shanghai, it has stuck to its principles. The capital of counter culture and inspiration for the likes of David Bowie and Iggy Pop has lost none of its radical, cutting edge reputation. Eastern wastelands are now "Ossi cool", where thousands of disused buildings have become squats for underground parties and art galleries.

Revival of the fittest

Planners are bringing back to life the wastelands that once scarred this capital of divided alliances. Not only is Berlin attempting to build a mini Manhattan in its business zones, a gentrified NYC TriBeCa in residential Mitte and a London with its new government buildings in Mitte and Tiergarten, but it is bravely facing up to its past by commemorating holocaust victims on land that had visually marked its urban and political dichotomy. It is also celebrating its past. The former Parliament is back in action and, though the royal family is not, their statues are back and their palaces are now open to all. Trams once ridiculed in the West as a noisy legacy of communism are quietly extending their routes all over the city. Only the Nazi era is buried and covered with the rubble that marked its final days. The height and size of Berlin's new buildings as well as the pedigree of their architects show the city has no doubt about its long-term future. Much of the 20th century will, in due course, be remembered by historians as a grim aberration. New generations will hopefully continue Berlin's pioneering spirit at the speed dictated by those in power in the 1990s.

Green revolution

Berlin is the greenest of cities – visually and politically. The Grunewald (Green Wood) is an enormous park to the southwest of the city, propping it up like the neck stem of the country's brain. The Green Party is in the ruling coalition, protecting the proud statistic that Berlin has more trees than shops, if not yet more bicycles than cars. Its buildings have more glass than concrete and solar energy powers them. Berliners are avid recyclers with drinkers returning bottles to shops and train users sorting rubbish into bins on platforms. But recycling is just one of many trends that starts as radical, spreads elsewhere and then almost becomes conservative. Gays came out in the 1920s and so did cyclists and nudists. By the time art causes a stir in London or New York it is conventional in Berlin. Take a look at the future here and see if you think it works.

At a glance

Mitte

For many tourists Mitte simply IS Berlin. Its greatest architectural achievements are all there and luxury has arrived in the shops and in the hotels. It is international with Germany playing a part, but a modest one on a very large canvas. Around Oranienburgerstrasse, home to the New Jewish Synagogue and Tacheles, one of the first art squats, the changes wrought in recent years have meant trendy bars and restaurants of an international flavour usurping grocery stores. It could be said it is losing its bohemian roots in favour of boutiques and strict club door codes. A more Berliner side of Mitte is seen in the streets behind. Where Auguststrasse and Linienstrasse strike parallel paths is *die schöne Viertel* (the beautiful quarter) as it abounds in all things beautiful. Visitors will now walk through the Brandenburg Gate to Tiergarten as they could not do so for nearly 30 years but in a way there is no need; Mitte has caught up and will not slip back.

Tiergarten

To the west is the Tiergarten, acres of woodland, grass, lakes and cycle tracks with only the occasional building as an intrusion. It is also home to people who would have been happy to see the former West Berlin stand still in 1985. Only on its fringes does the world move on. The Reichstag and surrounding new government buildings make it clear that Berlin is definitely the capital of Germany, if not of Europe, but these are deliberately shared with Mitte, across the River Spree, to stress the reunification. Only the Potsdamer Platz shared with Mitte gives it a truly contemporary feel.

Zehlendorf

To live in Zehlendorf is a sign of success and always has been. Houses built last year show this just as much as those built a hundred years ago. Everything is big in this rich, leafy quarter, but not ostentatious. It has been a broad-minded area too. Races and nationalities have mixed well, as have artistic and architectural styles. The Wannsee Lake is large enough to offer a beach, which is most welcome to tourists in the summer months.

Prenzlauerberg

This is the arty, bohemian centre of Berlin. Anything goes here and does. Other parts of Berlin are for the tame and the contented; Prenzlauerberg is for those in a hurry, for those who want to experiment, for those who want to change. Come here for ideas not for self-satisfaction. The latest fashionable bars, dark and retro, have gravitated towards Helmholzplatz. If a dress, a dish or a film catches on in Prenzlauerberg, see it next in London or Paris but nowhere else in Berlin. The neighbourhood had to be politically intense in the late 1980s when the East German Government could not face the thought of change, now central government concerns it less. Many people are self-employed here, few are unemployed, and it's the latest residential hotspot as families are now joining the singles who traditionally dominated the area.

Charlottenburg

Charlottenburg does not need to move with the times; it has shrugged off most previous regimes and will presumably continue to do so. It has money and it has time so it sees no need to keep open its shops late or to use convenience foods. Locals have a lengthy meal out or stay at home. They make no claims to be cosmopolitan when they have been so successful in a purely German environment. It seems pointless to build glass domes when the granite and marble of the 19th century are still intact. The opulent interior of the Charlottenburg Palace reflects the hold of the past on the surrounding area. Modern taste is to be kept firmly behind the doors of a few museums or a few restaurants. The vast parklands of Grunewald show similar staid tastes. Walk here, but do not leave litter, dress provocatively or expect any fun after sundown.

Friedrichshain

Also known as the new Prenzlauerberg it is far less attractive than its aspirational quarter with many more Communist era blocks and bleak buildings, but its gentrification, like other areas of the former East Berlin, is only a matter of time.

Kreuzberg and Schöneberg

Before reunification Kreuzberg in the then West Berlin was what Prenzlauerberg would have liked to have been. If the rest of the town was happy to enjoy its status as "the bulwark of freedom" and the seemingly never-ending *Wirtschaftswunder* (economic miracle) Kreuzberg was the power-house for new ideas and new people. It was bohemian in a way that few Germans could then cope with. It launched the protests against the Vietnam War in the 60s and then absorbed the Turkish immigrant communities in the 70s. It brought homosexuality out of the closet and is still a centre for the gay community. Politically it is still at the forefront of radical ideas; the artists, designers and dot.com fanatics who moved to Prenzlauerberg in the mid-90s did not take their politics with them. Expect the bars to have posters about the next demo rather than displays of protruding breasts and bottoms. It is the Turkish heart of Berlin and the second generation of Turks will probably determine the future of Kreuzberg. To the west is Schöneberg which has turned from alternative to up-market in recent years. There is still a young vibe to it and the main hub of the area is centred around Nollendorfplatz. With cafés like Berio and clubs like the KitKatClub this area is also popular with the gay community.

Around Berlin

Visitors to the palace at Potsdam, to the southwest of the city, will understand why the royal family when tired of Berlin, or frightened of it, were so happy there. Yet even Potsdam was insufficient for them; hence the palace at Köpenick to the east.

Trip planner

The weather in Berlin never matters; year-round it is easy to switch from indoors to outdoors and Berlin does not experience extremes of weather. When it is warm and sunny, take a long boat trip to Potsdam or to Köpenick. When it is cold and icy, take to your skates at the lakes around Grunewald. Hotel prices in Berlin work out very well for the tourist. They drop considerably at weekends, in July and August and at Christmas/New Year. There are a few annual trade fairs which you may want to avoid, since hotels and hostels both get full then. Check the dates of these fairs on www.berlin-tourism.de before making any plans.

24 hours

The Reichstag building beside the Brandenburg Gate is open from 0800 till 2400 so get up the cupola early for a preview and return late for a flood-lit retrospective. Take the No 100 bus along Unter den Linden, perhaps having the first coffee of the day at the Adlon Hotel before doing so. Get off at Bebelplatz to be surrounded by 19th-century Berlin. Cross the river and stroll left to the museums. Try to cover the Pergamon Museum and the Alte Nationalgalerie before a late lunch. Perhaps just make do with a filling snack from one of the many riverside sausage stands. Walk across the Schlossplatz where the East German parliament building is due for demolition during 2003, finally to be replaced by a rebuilt Royal Palace. Continue to the Gendarmenmarkt to see what rebuilding can do. Hopefully there will be an afternoon concert here in one of the cathedrals, which will provide an appropriate cultural interlude. A revived Friedrichstrasse is close by, ideal for stylish shops which have moved in from the West. Checkpoint Charlie of course no longer exists but it is commemorated on the Friedrichstrasse and, by following the fragment of the Wall still left, it is possible to reach ultra-modern Berlin at the Potsdamer Platz. Shiver for a few minutes as you walk past the excavated SS

★ **Ten of the best**

Best

1 Pergamon Museum German archaeologists returned from the ancient world with whole buildings and streets belonging to ancient Rome, Greece, Turkey and Babylon, p56.

2 The Story of Berlin Spying, terror, fear and finally celebration are all covered in this museum, p84.

3 Hamburger Bahnhof Don't expect to catch a train here. Do, however, expect shockingly nude paintings, floors covered in debris posing as sculpture, and other contemporary art, p67.

4 Reichstag The glass dome that forms part of the roof of the German Parliament was built by Sir Norman Foster. It is possible to listen to the debates, but much more fun is to look down from the top on new Berlin arising all around, p64.

5 Topography des Terrors A small open-air museum consisting simply of placards has been placed on top of the former SS Headquarters. Its name *The Topography of Terror* tells all. Some of the Berlin Wall also remains here, p99.

6 Alexanderplatz This large square was East Berlin's showcase. Whatever remained from before the war was cleared to build the best hotel, the best shops and the best cafés, p60.

7 Puschkinallee Guard Post Hundreds of similar towers used to surround West Berlin, and were used as look-outs for would-be escapers. This is the only one left as it was in 1989, p102.

8 Pfaueninsel (Peacock Island) Eccentric members of the Prussian royal family lived here, senior Nazis entertained here. Now the peacocks share their lawns with ordinary visitors, p106.

9 Adlon Hotel Afford a room if you can in Berlin's new heart, but otherwise linger over a beer as long as you dare in the lobby whilst the merely rich and the extremely rich flaunt by, p39.

10 Babelsberg Filmpark See how special effects were created before electronics could help and how American deserts survived the German winter, p118.

Headquarters. At the Potsdamer Platz, eat easily and ethnically both indoors and out of doors. A 10-minute walk brings you back to the Reichstag but if your night does not end until the morning, take the bus to Zoo Station where the neon lights and the bustle have always given Berlin its reputation as a 24-hour city.

A long weekend

First-time visitors coming for a short break will spend most of their days within a mile or so of the Brandenburg Gate. A walk along Unter den Linden and then a visit to Museumsinsel would make a good first day. If the weather is good, make a small detour en route to the Gendarmenmarkt for the first coffee of the day and then take a short break in the Lustgarten before visiting the museums. They all have spacious restaurants for lunch and for a second break take a short boat trip from the pier beside the Pergamon Museum.

The second day can be spent in the Kulturforum and the Potsdamer Platz. If absorbing the whole of German painting, not to mention the French, Spanish and British as well, takes up most of the day, leave the Potsdamer Platz until the evening and enjoy it illuminated. An alternative would be to go to the Berlin Philharmonic and catch up on Sir Simon Rattle's latest programme.

In the evening, perhaps stay in central Berlin; whether you return to the Gendarmenmarkt, amble along the Kurfürsten-damm or stick to Unter den Linden, you will get a meal of enormous proportions with unhurried, professional service. The same applies in hotels. Alternatively, make straight for Prenzlauerberg. Have a casual, early, Turkish meal and then allow plenty of time for the clubs.

The area around Charlottenburg Palace deserves a full day but a lot can be done in less. (If you are leaving from Tegel in the late afternoon, take your case with you, leave it at the cloakroom in the palace whilst you sightsee and then jump on the airport bus which stops in the Tegeler Weg and will reach the airport in only 10 minutes.) The palace and its gardens represent the best in 18th-

and 19th-century German architecture. The neighbouring museums and houses continue the story until the end of the 20th, and throw in Picasso's entire career as well. See how much Germany owes to individual philanthropists at the Bröhan Museum.

Remember that Monday is out for culture vultures as the large state and municipal museums are all closed together with the Charlottenburg and Potsdam palaces. The Monday "Ruhetag" (day of rest) is as sacrosanct to museums Sunday is to German shopkeepers on Sunday. However, politicos and gays need not worry since the Secret Police, Checkpoint Charlie, Story of Berlin, and Homosexual Museums are all open that day.

A week

The Americans were sensible when they chose Zehlendorf as their base during the occupation after the Second World War. The houses are bigger, lakes and woods are on the doorstep, the British did not bomb it and the Russians did not bombard it. Go west to enjoy here what few other capitals can offer – an island of peacocks, a rebuilt medieval village, the best of 1920s' art and even a beach. Further out is Potsdam; here the British did bomb ruthlessly and redundantly in April 1945, two weeks before the war ended, but the town has been restored and the palaces were untouched. From summer 2003, tourists will again go properly east, to celebrate the reopening of the Castle at Köpenick. As with Potsdam, try to go by boat. Have lunch on the way out, coffee and cake when there and dinner on the return journeyas Berlin lights up.

Contemporary Berlin

After reunification in 1990, the incorporation of East Berlin into the West was ruthless but effective. Bus routes, newspapers, postcodes and telephone numbers all expanded east and nothing went in the opposite direction. Western developers saw the potential along Friedrichstrasse and beside the former Wall and seized it. They did not wait for the formal government decision in June 1991 that Berlin would again be the capital of Germany. They had taken this for granted 18 months before.

Since reunification the dice have been loaded in favour of one side. The West had enjoyed massive subsidies from Bonn and once these ended, corners had to be cut. Easterners expected an instant transformation to the standards of the West and were not ready for the seamier side of a capitalist economy and particularly not for unemployment. Senior posts in all fields went to "Wessies" rather than to "Ossies" - a political past in the GDR was seen as a danger to the future of the city. Although the PDS, the socialist party based in the east, has sometimes won enough seats to be included in the ruling coalition, it has never had real power. This has always stayed with the parties that grew up in the West. Today it pays to be young and to have had no career in former East Berlin.

Another problem continuing to plague Berlin is that business has been slow to take it more seriously. The arrival of the government from Bonn in 1999 turned out to be more of a damp squib than a panacea. Business stayed rooted in Hamburg, Frankfurt and Munich and, incredibly, the city still needs to persuade the national airline, Lufthansa, to provide a direct flight to America. But things may be looking up. The announcement in autumn 2002 that Coca Cola's European headquarters would move to Berlin may encourage other large corporations to do the same and though Frankfurt is now home for the European Central Bank, the Deutsche Bank has at least shown its commitment to Berlin by rebuilding its headquarters on their old site beside the Brandenburg Gate. The beginning of EU

High design
A symphony of glass and steel make up the Sony Center at the heart of the Potsdamer Platz

expansion in 2004 will also see Berlin once more at the crossroads of eastern and western Europe, and perhaps allow the grand Deutsche dame to take her place centre stage.

Architects appear to have had more faith in the German capital and in the past decade architecture has finally been separated from politics. Sometimes, as with the Reichstag, there is a frame to work with, so a 19th-century surround gets a 21st-century cupola from Sir Norman Foster. When the addition IM Pei (famous for the Louvre pyramid) designed for the 18th century German History Museum is completed, this will complement one of Berlin's earliest buildings. Elsewhere, as in the Potsdamer Platz, there was nothing to rebuild, so planners could start from scratch with the vaguest of briefs - to stress unity and activity in an area that had been bleak and divided for 30 years. They have, as a result, built a variety of skyscrapers interspersed with wide pedestrian precincts and plenty of fountains.

Despite the progress, however, Berlin is less than optimistic about the future. Indeed, Berlin-bashing has become all the rage in the media. The words *pleite* (bankrupt) and *schmuddelig* (messy) constantly appear in the local papers, which report at length on the 900 cafés that closed in the previous year, while ignoring the 800 that opened. Part of the reason, of course, is that Berlin as the country's capital is now more closely associated with national government. When Gerhard Schröder's government scraped in by a whisker in September 2002 and then faced immediate unpopularity, Berlin felt sure it would suffer likewise. The German press feels nervous about its capital city yet indifferent to similar problems in Frankfurt, Hamburg or Munich. But visitors to the city will be surprised to learn of its low self-esteem. Most will only see the affluent areas around the centre and in the western suburbs en route to Potsdam. Even if they venture east to the grim tower blocks of Marzhan they will see far less poverty than at home.

Visitors from outside of Europe will find it quaint that Berlin has no long-haul links, so passengers from North America and Australasia still have to change planes in Copenhagen, Frankfurt or London. Europeans, however, are now very well served with a multitude of different airlines flying into three city airports, an ever-faster rail service and good coach links.

Public transport within Berlin is superb, as much in the city centre as in the distant suburbs. Trams with two coaches and double-decker buses cope well even with rush-hour traffic. The over- and underground train services remain of course immune to traffic elsewhere. The network is increasing all the time, leaving little need for taxis or private cars, both of which exist in abundance.

Getting there

Air

From the UK For British travellers, air is the only sensible way to reach Berlin. Direct flights from London, Birmingham and Manchester operate several times a day, but Scotland still has no direct link to Berlin, so travel from there has to be via Amsterdam or another UK airport. Londoners are spoilt for choice with flights leaving from London City, Gatwick, Heathrow and Stansted. Most serve Tegel Airport in the western part of Berlin, but the budget airlines from Stansted usually fly to Schönefeld, to the southeast of the city. A few flights go to Templehof, including one from London City. It is the airport closest to the city centre but which has the fewest regular services. It is worth seeing just for the terminal, one of the few buildings in Berlin bequeathed by the Nazi era. In 2007, it is hoped Schönefeld will have expanded sufficiently to take all the air traffic for Berlin, and the other two airports will then close. **Air Berlin** flies to Tegel and **Ryanair**, which has taken over the former **buzz** route, will fly from 1 May 2003 (see box p23) to Schönefeld. Fares can be as low as £40 return. Fares vary very little throughout the year, but fewer rock-bottom fares are offered over Christmas, Easter and around trade fairs. Now that scheduled carriers have decided to fight back, they often offer comparable fares to those of the low-cost carriers. For a ticket on a scheduled airline between the UK and Berlin, it should normally be possible to travel for around £150 return.

From Europe Most European capitals have direct flights to Berlin, as do the larger cities in western Germany. Berlin followed Frankfurt as a target for low-cost airlines but now has an increasing number of these services on both domestic and international routes. For example, **Ryanair** (see box, p23) flies within Germany. Fares from other parts of Germany can be €50 return. Always check airport taxes when booking; they vary greatly from airport to airport so a different routing may well save considerable sums of money. For those with time and patience, searching websites will probably provide the cheapest source of airfares on their own. However, buying tickets through travel agents will not cost much more and could well cost less when included as part of a package.

From North America There are very few long-haul flights to Berlin so travellers from America and Asia have to change planes en route, usually in Western Europe. Fares of US$600 round trip from the East Coast are available for much of the year but expect to pay much more in mid-summer and over Christmas/New Year. Always check taxes before booking and see how they compare with those from a neighbouring airport.

Airport information www.berlin-airport.de covers all three Berlin airports. It has terminal plans, schedules, arrival/departure information and details of public transport links. It will work out routes from each airport within the city. Airport information also from **T** 0180 50 00 186.

　Tegel airport has one terminal; a check-in desk and departure area is allocated to each flight. There are no toilets airside. The airport has a BVG office. **BVG**, the Berlin transport authority, runs all buses, trains and trams in Berlin and Potsdam. Their Tipinfo guide will provide an instant printed routing to any address in the city with the timings included. Explanations are in English. The office sells travel passes (see Getting Around, p29) and individual tickets; it also has free leaflets.

　The **Berlin Tourismus Marketing**, the Berlin Tourist Board, has an information counter close to the BVG one, and can book

! Tegel airport was originally called Otto Lilienthal and must have been unique in being named after an airline pioneer who was fatally injured in a plane he had built. This was in 1898 and standards have greatly improved since then.

Airlines and tour operators

Air Berlin, www.airberlin.com, **T** 0870 738 8880 (UK)
British Airways, www.ba.com, **T** 0845 773 3377 (UK)
Germanwings, www.germanwings.com, **T** 020 8321 7255 (UK)
KLM, www.klm.com, **T** 0870 507 4074 (UK)
Lufthansa, www.lufthansa.com, **T** 0845 773 7747 (UK)
Ryanair/buzz, www.ryanair.com, www.buzzaway.com,
T 0870 240 7070 (Ryanair, UK)

German National Tourist Office, www.germany-tourism.de,
T 020 7317 0908 (UK)
Kirker Holidays, www.kirkerholidays.com, **T** 020 7231 3333 (UK)
Martin Randall Architecture Tours, www.martinrandall.com,
T 020 8742 3355 (UK)
Osprey Holidays, www.osprey-holidays.co.uk, **T** 0845 601
0703 (UK)
Regent Holidays, www.Regent-holidays.co.uk, **T** 0117 921
1711 (UK)
Travelscene, www.travelscene.co.uk, **T** 0870 010 2180 (UK)

hotel rooms and give details of sightseeing tours. See also Tourist
information, p33.

Buses No X9 and No 109 are the choice of most travellers
leaving the airport since they pass most areas where hotels
are located. No 128 is better for those heading north or east.
All pass many U-Bahn stations but the U-Bahn itself does not
serve Tegel. No 109 takes 30 minutes to reach Zoo Station, the
No X9 about 20 minutes as it makes fewer stops. The TXL express
bus goes to Mitte. One-way tickets (€2.10) are valid for two
hours so cover transfers. The airport closes overnight so there
are no problems with public transport, which always covers
the earliest departures and the latest arrivals.

Taxis are all metered and are plentiful at the airport. A taxi from Tegel will cost about €20 to Zoo Station, about €30 to Mitte. A tip of 5-10% is normal.

The Essbahn is the best place to linger when a flight is delayed. It is outside the terminal, beside the departure point for buses into town. The name is a pun on the German word "essen" which means "to eat" and S-Bahn which is the name of the overground railway. The café operates from a converted railway carriage and serves spiced-up German food. Come here for a curry or salsa sausage before the milder in-flight catering.

Templehof airport is always on the verge of closure but somehow survives. It specializes in short-haul flights within Germany and the occasional service further afield. It is the most central of the three and the only one with a U-Bahn station nearby– Platz der Luftbrücke. It is on line 6 which goes to Friedrichstrasse station (15 minutes' journey). Five bus routes also serve the airport. A taxi to Friedrichstrasse would cost €15. There is no tourist office.

Schönefeld airport. When this becomes Berlin-Brandenburg airport in 2007 it should be a very different place from what it is now. The railway will come right into the terminals, and there will be an express service reaching central Berlin in 15 minutes. For now, the links are rather tortuous. A shuttle bus links the terminal with the S-Bahn station Schönefeld which is also on the main line to the east. Trains into town take about 40 minutes. Eight bus routes link the airport with southern and eastern Berlin. The No 171 goes to Rudow, the final station on U-Bahn line 7 which heads for the northwest. There are two night buses and the S-Bahn also runs at night on this route. A taxi to Friedrichstrasse costs €40. There is no tourist office.

! Lufthansa was banned from flying to Berlin until 1990; only the airlines of the four "victors" in the Second World War had this right for the preceding 40 years.

Train

Express trains (**ICE**) link Berlin with all major German cities. The journey to Frankfurt takes 3½ hours, to Hamburg about 2 hours, and to Hanover 1½ hours. International journeys take rather longer as high-speed trains do not yet operate on these routes. Brussels takes more than 7 hours and Paris nearly 9 hours. Changing trains in Brussels from **Eurostar** (www.eurostar.com) gives a journey time of around 10 hours from London. Most long-distance trains leave from Zoo Station, a few from Ostbahnhof. The previously insignificant Lehrter Bahnhof, between Zoo and Friedrichstrasse, is now being converted into a major station and office complex. By 2006 it will be Berlin's main station for travel in all directions. Fares are higher on the ICE trains than on slower ones but a wide variety of travel passes are available from travel agents accredited to German Railways (**Deutsche Bahn**, www.bahn.de). These are not of much use for travel within Berlin, but can be used in conjunction with onward travel and also for day trips to, say, Dresden or Leipzig. German Railways have an excellent website (see above), which is kept constantly up to date on timetables, fares and travel passes. In Zoo Station there is a special ticket office for English- speakers, EurAide, which is situated between the main hall and the luggage lockers. It is open daily in the summer but not on Saturday afternoon or Sunday during the winter (1 October 1-31 March).

Road

With the speed of the trains and the reduced cost of air travel, coach travel has lost much of its appeal but the fact that bus companies allow reservation changes gives travel this way greater flexibility than on the cheaper air and rail tickets. The coach station (Zentralomnibusbahnhof, known as ZOB) is right beside the ICC Conference Centre on Masurenallee. International and domestic timetables from **Berlin Linien Bus** (www.berlinlinienbus.de).

Travel extras

Costs Berliners quickly called the Euro a "Teuro" when it was introduced in January 2002, punning on the German word "teuer" which means expensive. In fact, with a little planning, tourism can be very cheap. The museums and transport authorities have got together to produce travel cards which cover all admission fees and the use of the extensive bus, tram and rail network. Kiosks abound with filling snacks and drinks; if menu prices in some restaurants look daunting, take account of the size of the dish. Few people take three courses in Berlin, some take only one.

Safety The level of street crime in Berlin is similar to that in London and Paris. Care should be taken on station platforms and on crowded buses. Violent crime is fortunately rare.

There is little point in driving to Berlin unless a parking place has been booked in advance or accommodation is in the distant suburbs where street parking is still easily available and free of charge. Drivers should remember it is illegal to drive in Germany without carrying a driving licence.

Getting around

Bus

Bus No 100 is without doubt the favourite of all tourists as it links most of the major sites in the centre. It starts at Zoo Station and then makes its way eastwards to Alexanderplatz, passing beside the Victory Column, the Reichstag, the Brandenburg Gate, and then along Unter den Linden to Museumsinsel. Continue to Prenzlauerberg and explore this revived artistic quarter.

The No 129 also starts at Zoo Station and passes KaDeWe, the most famous Berlin department store, before a long drive beside the Landwehr Canal. It crosses the canal to pass the ruin of Anhalter Station, Berlin's most famous before the Second World War. Next it comes to the former Checkpoint Charlie, a regular flashpoint during the Cold War. This is the place to get off before it then proceeds to the eastern suburbs. The No 110 offers a leisurely way to reach Zehlendorf from Zoo Station as it drives along the entire length of the Kurfürstendamm and then through the affluent suburb of Grunewald before reaching its destination.

The bus network at night is almost as extensive as that by day. The BVG has free leaflets detailing all the services, and timetables are on every relevant bus stop. In the suburbs, drivers will, if requested, phone ahead for a taxi to meet the bus, when passengers have concerns about their safety.

Car

As Berlin has much wider streets than most other European capitals, driving around it is not quite so ludicrous as it might appear. Trying to stop en route would be rash, as there are few parking meters and even fewer garages but the major sites could be seen within 2-3 hours and in the summer nature can be enjoyed by driving through the Tiergarten and along the rivers and canals. A car is ideal for Potsdam and nearby attractions such as the Babelsberg Filmpark, and except at summer weekends, parking is not too difficult. For car hire information, see p214.

Cycling

Berlin is perfect for cycling. There is no serious hill within the entire city limits, and very few in the neighbouring countryside. All the major roads in the town centre have cycle tracks, usually on the pavement rather than on the road and there are many others through the parks and beside the canals and lakes.

Little unites the Weimar Republic of the 1920s with the subsequent Nazi and communist eras, but cycling certainly does. It has always been taken seriously in Germany. With the reopening of the Brandenburg Gate in 2002, it remained uncertain what traffic would be allowed through. The only point of agreement was permission for cyclists to do this. Bikes can be taken on the S-Bahn at all times and on the U-Bahn outside rush hours. An extra ticket or travel card is necessary for the bike.

Taxi

These are plentiful, if largely unnecessary, for most tourists. There are ranks at most U-Bahn and S-Bahn stations in the suburbs, and they can easily be hailed in the town centre. There are also ranks around the Potsdamer Platz and at the Brandenburg Gate. Prices start around €2 with a charge of around €1 per kilometre. A minimal tip is appreciated, but not expected. All licensed taxis have a very clear taxi sign on them. Gypsy taxis are fortunately almost unheard of in Berlin.

U-Bahn and S-Bahn

It is a pity to take the S-Bahn or U-Bahn for most journeys in Berlin. With one or two exceptions, the best views are missed but the extensive network does of course offer very fast travel all over the city. The S-Bahn goes further, to Potsdam in the west and to Schönefeld Airport in the southeast. Most stations have lifts as well as stairs and escalators, so use by the disabled and those with buggies/strollers is relatively straightforward.

Two U-Bahn lines operate at night, the U9 going from north to south and the U12 going from west to east. Both serve Zoo Station. The S-Bahn service S7 also runs all night, going from Potsdam in the west through Charlottenburg, past Zoo Station and Friedrichstrasse to the eastern backwater of Ahrensfelde.

Walking

For walkers, Berlin is still two cities. Itineraries start either around Zoo Station in the west or in Friedrichstrasse in the east. The only combination would be to start at the Reichstag and to follow the old border to Potsdamer Platz. With public transport being so

Travel passes

BVG, the Berlin Transport Authority, runs all buses, trams, underground and surface railways within Berlin and to neighbouring areas such as Potsdam. The U-Bahn runs underground and the S-Bahn runs overground but also has long sections underground as well.

The city is divided into three travel zones, A, B, and C. Visitors are only likely to travel in zone C if they visit Potsdam. A single ticket valid for any number of journeys within two hours cost €2.10. Day passes for zones A and B combined cost €6.10 and 7-day ones cost €22.00. To add zone C, the costs increase to €6.30 and €28.

Tickets and passes are available at the Tegel Airport office, at the BVG enquiry centre outside Zoo Station on the Hardenberg-platz and from machines on all station platforms and from ticket offices at larger stations. Bus and tram drivers only sell single tickets, not passes. Day and night fares are the same.

Up-to-date information on schedules and fares: www.bvg.de
For combined travel and museum passes, see box, p32.

good, there is no need to commit in advance to any particular routing. A bus or a train will always be within a hundred yards should the weather change or tiredness set in.

Pedestrians are respected in Germany, if not quite as much as cyclists, then sufficiently for wide pavements to be provided and separate signposts to be erected. However, jaywalking is strictly forbidden; never wander into a street except at a marked crossing and also wait for the green light, even in the middle of the night when there may well be no traffic.

Tours

Architectural tours

An architectural tour can be taken using S-Bahn lines S3, S5, S7 and S9 between Charlottenburg in the west and Alexanderplatz in the east. To begin with, there is little sign of bombing and rebuilding, but around Zoo Station, the town is totally new. Passing through Tiergarten gives a glimpse of the Victory Monument before coming to Lehrter Stadtbahnhof, a small station soon to become Berlin's biggest. Crossing the River Spree offers views of the new government quarter around the Reichstag and then the many buildings left from East German times. After Friedrichstrasse, there are views of Museumsinsel, the "Red" Town Hall and the Nikolai quarter. Alexanderplatz is still in the communist 1970s. It desperately needs a face-lift.

Boat tours

Berlin must be one of few capitals where boat trips are more varied than those by coach. A circle trip can be made which combines the Spree River and Landwehr Canal. In the centre, this is the best way of seeing Museumsinsel and the new government quarter which is deliberately spread across the Spree River since at that point it had been the border between East and West Berlin. It is also a convenient way of seeing how much of 19th-century Berlin has in fact been preserved and how much industry there still is.

Longer trips reach Potsdam along the Spree and then Havel rivers. Trips start from the piers at the Pergamon Museum, Jannowitzbrücke S-Bahn station and fromthe Estrel Hotel. They cannot be prebooked and the commentary is only in German, although written texts in English are handed out. Timetables and prices are listed at each pier but can be checked on www.reederei-riedel.de, the website of **Shipping Company Riedel** that runs the tours.

Coach tours

Sightseeing tours have a large number of different departure points so these need to be checked when booking. Some of these pick up at the large hotels. They all have a departure point near to Zoo Station and another on the Alexanderplatz.

General sightseeing tours by coach usually take around 3 hours and travel along the Kurfürstendamm before turning north to the Charlottenburg Palace. They return to the centre via the Victory Column and Bellevue Castle. Stops are made at the Reichstag and the Brandenburg Gate before heading south to the Potsdamer Platz. After a stop at Checkpoint Charlie, they drive along Friedrichstrasse to Unter den Linden where they turn east to Museumsinsel and the Town Hall. It is also possible to take two half-day sightseeing tours, one in the west and one in the east. A short trip to Potsdam can be done in a half-day which includes a visit to Sans Souci Palace but to see the gardens and other palaces properly, a full day is needed there. A number of firms operate these tours and all can be booked at the offices of Berlin Tourismus Marketing (see p33).

Cycle tours

The best place to hire bikes and do bike tours is the **Fahrrad-station** at Friedrichstrasse U-Bahn/S-Bahn station in Mitte. From summer 2003, it will also run cycle tours of Berlin, with English-speaking guides. The website is www.fahrradstation.de but, at the time of writing, it is only in German. See also Directory, p214.

Potsdam tours

Tours are often based in Potsdam as a visit to all the palaces and the restored town centre can easily last several days. However, much can be done within a day: a tour can start at Sans Souci Palace with some time allowed for the gardens and outlying buildings; continue to Cecilienhof Palace before returning for some time in the town centre. Sans Souci and the New Palace can only

Travel and museum passes

The Berlin Tourismus Marketing, see p33, has a 3-day **Welcome Card** for €19 which covers travel in all 3 travel zones and offers considerable discounts on admission charges to museums, theatres and sightseeing tours. Alternatively the 3-day **Schaulust** (meaning desire to see) costs €10 and provides free admission to all state museums but no other concessions.

Many museums close on Monday, but among those that do not are the Bauhaus Archiv, Brücke Museum, Haus am Checkpoint Charlie, Jüdisches Museum, Käthe-Kollwitz-Museum, Story of Berlin and Topographie des Terrors.

The fashionable time to visit museums is on the twice-yearly "**Lange Nacht der Museen**" (Long Museum Night) when most stay open until 0200 and special bus routes are created to link them. This is usually on the last Saturday in January and August (www.lange-nacht-der-museem.de). A €12 ticket covers admission and free travel from 1500 on Saturday until 0500 on Sunday. For up to date information check the website www. Mdberlin.de For more background on the larger state museums see www.smpk.de

Once in Berlin, buy the monthly *Berlin Programm* which gives current opening hours, fees and details of all temporary exhibitions. State museums such as those on Museumsinsel, the Charlottenburg Palace, and the Kulturforum galleries charge €6 for a day card which allows admission into all these collections and smaller municipal ones. There are no tickets sold just for one of these museums so it is worthwhile to visit several in one day. During 2003 the Köpenick castle will reopen and this ticket will be valid there too. Admission is free to all these collections on the first Sunday of the month. For those not buying this card, the municipal museums have individual charges (usually around €1.50) and many are free of charge on Wednesdays.

be visited on guided tours, some of which are organized in English. As they both open at 0900, it is advisable in the summer to arrive early to be sure of a place. All the buildings in Potsdam are closed on Mondays, although the gardens are open daily until sunset. See also p111. A variety of combination tickets for various buildings can be bought at the tourist office, see p34. Some of these also include castles elsewhere in Brandenburg province and the Babelsberg Filmpark.

Walking tours
A wide selection of walking tours is available in English, many centred on specific periods of history or around certain themes such as the U-Bahn, Literary Berlin or modern architecture. One firm that caters exclusively for English-speaking visitors is **Berlin Walks**. Among the themes they cover are "Infamous Third Reich Sites", "Jewish Life in Berlin" and "Discover Potsdam". The tours operate year-round in all weathers. Some use public transport for short journeys. These tours are for real enthusiasts. Full details of the programme from **T** 30 19 194, www.berlinwalks.com

Tourist information

Berlin Tourismus Marketing, **T** 25 00 25, www.berlin-tourism.de, is the local tourist board and has offices in the Europa-Center at Budapesterstrasse 45 (open 1 November to 31 March, Monday to Saturday 1000-1900, Sunday 1000-1800, 1 April to 31 October, extended opening hours), at the Brandenburg Gate (open daily 1 November-31 March, 1000-1800, 1 April-31 October, extended opening hours) and at the Television Tower at Alexanderplatz (open daily 1 November-31 March, 1000-1800, 1 April-31 October, extended opening hours). These have a wide range of free introductory leaflets to the city.

The office can also book hotels, sightseeing tours, river trips and they have a tasteful selection of souvenirs for sale. It also operates a Berlin hotline: **T** 0049-700 TOBERLIN (862 37 546), Monday-Friday 0800-1900, Saturday and Sunday 0900-1800.

The Potsdam tourist office is at Friedrich-Ebertstrasse 5, **T** 0331 27 55 80, **F** 0331 27 55 899, www.potsdam.de From April until October they are open Monday-Friday 0900-2000, Saturday-Sunday 0900-1600. In winter they are open during the week from 1000 until 1800 and at weekends from 1000 until 1400. Given the varying opening hours of the different palaces and the variety of admission tickets, it is well worth checking their website before coming to Potsdam.

Mitte

The literal translation of Mitte is "middle" but "heart" is so much more appropriate. In the first half of the 20th century it was almost self-contained when all that mattered in German history, art, government, diplomacy and fun took place within its confines. It had a less certain role in East German times. When it was in East Berlin it was missed more than any ordinary city centre would have been and no amount of building and renewal in the West could replace it.

*After reunification, developers moved in with a vengeance, and it was soon difficult to distinguish new buildings here from their counterparts in the West. The public sector was, however, not too far behind. Once again, visitors come to see the **Pergamon Museum** and its neighbours on **Museumsinsel**, the elegant town houses of the **Nikolaiviertel**, and above all to enjoy passing through the **Brandenburg Gate**, which had not been possible for 30 years. They can enjoy concerts at all the reconsecrated **cathedrals** too. Along **Unter den Linden** is the **Adlon Hotel** and the **Russian Embassy**; further east are the **Humboldt-Universität**, **Bebelplatz** and the **Deutsche Historische Museum**.*

▸▸ *See Sleeping p124, Eating and drinking p142, Bars and clubs, p161*

◉ Sights

★ Brandenburger Tor (Brandenburg Gate)
Pariser Platz. *S-Bahn Unter den Linden. Map 7, F1, p254*

Built in 1791 at the western end of Pariser Platz, the happiest and saddest days of Berlin's history have all been played out here. Conquerors from abroad such as Napoleon had to seize the quadriga from the top of the gate in order to humiliate the local population, which he did in 1806. (After his defeat, the Prussian army brought it back from Paris in 1814.) Conquerors from within such as Hitler organized their first march-pasts here to show the future irrelevance of all democratic institutions. On 30 January 1933, the Nazis organized a three-hour long torchlight parade through the gate. Their regime surrendered to the Russians around it in May 1945. On 17 June 1953 East German workers paraded through it to protest at the lower wages the government was trying to impose on builders. To stem the flow of refugees westward, the East German Government had in 1961 to build the Wall in front of the gate which isolated it for 28 years.

Since 9 November 1989, the day the border was reopened, television stations use every possible occasion to show film of young people from both sides of the border climbing onto the Wall in front of the gate to drink champagne.

The gate was restored between 2000 and 2002. Among other repairs, the bullet holes left from 1945 were filled in. The gate was unveiled again on 3 October 2002, the 12th anniversary of German reunification, in front of former US President Clinton who proclaimed it to be "now a symbol of unity, not of division".

Pariser Platz
S-Bahn Unter den Linden. Map 7, F2, p254

No building will be taller than the Brandenburg Gate and none will have excessive glass when all structures here are completed in 2005. The square was a wilderness during the division as it was too close to the Wall for building to be allowed. The American Embassy will return to the south side now that the State Department and German town planners have worked out a compromise between the needs of security and the needs of the environment. The Academy of Fine Arts will be beside it.

The French Embassy reopened on the north side in early 2003, together with a residential block, named after its most famous pre-war resident, the artist Max Liebermann. He was President of the Academy of Fine Arts until sacked by the Nazis as a Jew in May 1933. He was lucky to die in 1935 of natural causes and was able to stay in his flat on the square until his death.

Denkmal für die ermordeten Juden (Memorial to the murdered Jews)
S-Bahn Unter den Linden. Map 7, G2, p254

It may be 2005 before the Holocaust Memorial is completed. The site and design were agreed in 1999, but work is unlikely to start before late 2003 at the earliest. It is about 200 yards from the Brandenburg Gate, towards Potsdamer Platz, on land just to the east of the former border. The location had to be central, but not too close to any site associated with the Nazis. This was the compromise. It is a bleak empty space at present, but in due course it will be covered by a "forest of stelae" representing grave stones which all those murdered were denied.

Adlon Hotel
Pariser Platz. *S-Bahn Unter den Linden. Map 7, F2, p254*

From the outside, the Adlon Hotel has never looked more than a solidly built office and the architects Carl Gause and Robert Leipniz are now hardly remembered. But, from 1907 when it opened, nobody would forget any aspect of the interior, whether it was the bronze beds, Carrara marble staircase or the "Sauce diable" hurriedly invented here for Edward VII.

Through two world wars it managed to ignore rationing, bombing and political correctness. In September 1939, it "imprisoned" British and French diplomats until the Swiss could

! "I cannot eat enough to produce sufficient vomit." Artist Max Liebermann as he saw the Nazi parade beneath his window on 30 January 1933.

Rebel with a cause

Max Liebermann (1847-1935) was lucky to live and die when he did. Perhaps one can call him a "secessionist" as that was the school of painting to which he stayed close, but he was above all a rebel in what he painted and what he said.

He enjoyed teasing and provoking; he painted at just the time when such behaviour was acceptable both on canvas and in salons. His arrogance was so outrageous it was hilarious. He cultivated a coarse Berlin accent, particularly inappropriate for his prestigious address in a house beside the Brandenburg Gate.

His last two years, under the Nazi regime, were a time of great physical and emotional pain, but he did at least die of natural causes, which might well not have been the case had he lived much longer.

If his paintings seem too "ernst" (serious), remember the following quotes from him: "If you look at a Frans Hals, you want to start to paint, but if you look at a Rembrandt, you want to give up." On being asked if he prepared his sketches with a hard or a soft pencil, he replied: "merely with talent".

One potential sitter asked him to come to the house first to see how the portrait would best fit around the other paintings and the furniture. Liebermann told her she should rebuild the house to fit his picture, not the other way round. When visiting the studio of fellow artist Lovis Corinth, he exclaimed: "What, do you need to use a rubber?" On the role of art historians: "When we are dead, they are useful in denying the provenance of all our lousy paintings and crediting us just with our masterpieces."

transport them out of Germany. Staff ensured the wine cellar was emptied a few hours before the Russians seized it in 1945.

Unter den Linden and Britische Botschaft (British Embassy)
Wilhelmstr. *S-Bahn Unter den Linden.* *Map 7, F2, p254*

Unter den Linden (Amongst the Lime Trees) is one of very few streets in Berlin to have kept its name over the centuries. Hitler cut down the trees to accommodate his parades but otherwise they have always stayed too. It runs eastwards from the Brandenburg Gate and Pariser Platz. The trees in the centre now make a congenial pedestrian precinct between the two wide traffic lanes on either side. The first street to the south is the **Wilhelmstrasse** and the first building on the right is the British Embassy designed by British architect Michael Wilford (of Lowry fame). In East German times, the embassy was in Unter den Linden but on reunification it reclaimed its former site. It breaks from traditional embassy design in every way possible. With its varied uses of colours and glass, it invites and does not overawe. It has a cafeteria, computer room, light boxes and sandstone sculptures. Only two items are linked with the past – the wrought iron gates from the pre-war embassy which are displayed on the staircase and the oak-tree in the courtyard which is 50 years old.

Russische Botschaft (Russian Embassy)
Unter den Linden. *S-Bahn Unter den Linden.* *Map 7, F3, p254*

Walking east along Unter den Linden, after crossing Wilhelmstrasse, this is the first building on the south side. Built by the Soviets immediately after the Second World War, they were not bothered by planning regulations and centuries of practice along Unter den Linden. As a result, they did not have a straight front façade nor did they limit the building to the usual six stories. The building is better than most examples of socialist realism but now seems totally incongruous in a Berlin eager to forget its links with the former USSR.

Friedrichstrasse Station
Friedrichstr. S-Bahn and U-Bahn Friedrichstr. Map 7, D4, p254

Friedrichstrasse station (1934-38) is one of the few buildings left
in Berlin with an exterior dating from the Nazi period. The interior
was completely changed in 1961 when it became one of the few
border crossings to West Berlin. To the north of the station, the
building on the western side of Friedrichstrasse was for crying
and that on the eastern side for laughing. The **Palace of Tears
(Tränenpalast)**, as it came to be known, was the building used
for the stringent passport controls carried out before passengers
could catch the trains for West Berlin. It is now a concert hall but
it has taken on this name officially. On the other side of the road,
the **Distel** (thistle) is a political cabaret venue. It functioned with
considerable freedom in East German times and the political
temperature of the time could usually be judged by how critical
the acts were of the government.

Gendarmenmarkt
U-Bahn Stadtmitte. Map 7, G6, p254

If there is still a tendency to judge Germany by the worst periods
of its history, a stop in this square will show the country at its most
liberal. It became the centre of a French community around 1700
when Prussia gave refuge to 6,000 persecuted Huguenots. The
Französischer Dom (French Cathedral), on the north side of the
square, dates from this time, as does the **Deutscher Dom** built to
similar proportions on the south side. Both have been extended
and rebuilt on several occasions since then, but the symmetry has
always been maintained. The French one is still used for worship,
but the German one houses an exhibition which used to be in the
Reichstag before unification. Despite its austere title – "Questions
on German History" – it is in fact a wide-ranging collection of
documents and pictures dating from 1800 until the present.

★ **Berlin breathers**

- On a boat meandering along the Spree
- On the lawns of Peacock Island
- On the top deck of a No 200 bus
- On a bicycle through the Tiergarten
- At the Philharmonie even if Sir Simon Rattle is not conducting

The **Konzerthaus** (Concert hall) in the centre is still often referred to by its earlier name **Schauspielhaus** (Playhouse). The original was built in 1800 but was destroyed by fire in 1817. Its replacement was one of the earliest buildings by Karl Friedrich Schinkel (1781-1841), see box, p47, who would then be responsible for so many more in this part of Berlin. He took on the task of making his replacement fire-proof. This it was, although it could not of course withstand bomb damage 130 years later.

In front of the concert hall is a statue of one of Germany's most famous writers, Friedrich Schiller (1759-1805). The Nazis removed it in 1936 to a store in what would become West Berlin and it was only returned to the east in 1986 when very limited co-operation took place between both regimes as they planned their separate celebrations of Berlin's 750th birthday for 1987. The square is often used for open-air concerts in the summer.

● *The best view of the square is from the tower of the French Cathedral.*

Bebelplatz
U-Bahn Französische Str. Map 7, F6, p254

Bebelplatz is one of the few name changes implemented in East German times which has stuck, probably because August Bebel was a 19th-century social democrat respected throughout Germany. Before the war it was Opernplatz (Opera Square) and

★ **Places to stand**

Best

• On the roof of the Reichstag at twilight, p64
• In front of the Pergamon Temple, p56
• At a hamburger stand overlooking Museumsinsel
• On top of the "burning books" at The Story of Berlin, p84
• On the platform at U-Bahn Station Märkisches Museum where murals of old Berlin replace the advertisements

that name will always be associated with the **Burning of the Books** that took place here on 10 May 1933. Nazi soldiers raided the nearby library of Magnus Hirschfeld which held about 20,000 books. Being Jewish, a social democrat and homosexual, he was an instant Nazi target. The entire library was publicly and enthusiastically destroyed in the presence of Joseph Goebbels, Hitler's propaganda minister. German artistic creativity died that night. A large sheet of glass in place of a paving stone commemorates this; beneath it are rows of empty bookshelves. Beside it is a quotation from poet Heinrich Heine, who seemed to predict Nazism over 100 years before it came to power: "Where books are burnt, humans will also suffer the same fate."

In a much happier vein, the square and its surroundings commemorate the co-operation between Frederick the Great and his architect Georg von Knobelsdorff giving rise to the name Forum Fridericianum being used to describe the area.

On the western side of the square is the **Alte Bibliothek** which was the Royal Library. Berliners, who like to find nicknames for all their famous buildings, call this one the "Chest of Drawers" and it is not hard to see why. It is now part of the University.

The **Staatsoper** (National Opera House) on the eastern side was the largest in Europe when built and the front entrance was reserved for the King. He in fact planned it with Knobelsdorff before he even ascended the throne. It originally had 2,000 seats but only royal guests were invited. The public had to wait until after Frederick the Great's death to be admitted. The building was one of the first to be bombed during the war, in 1941, and because of Hitler's interest in Frederick, he had it immediately rebuilt. This was to no avail, as it was destroyed again in 1944 but it would be faithfully restored in the early 1950s.

Bundesministerium für Verkehr, Bau-und Wohnungswesen (The Ministry of Transport, Building and Housing)

Bebelplatz, **T** 20 08 30 60. *Daily 0900-1700. Free. U-Bahn Hausvogteiplatz. Map 7, F6, p254*

This is a building hardly visited by foreigners. It has a large model of Berlin before the war and temporary exhibitions about future building plans for the city. Half an hour here will give a far better impression of what Berlin was and what it will be than days spent reading books. Berlin was at its architectural best in the 1920s and it will be another 10 years or so before we can judge whether the completed modern city is a worthy successor of what is seen here.

St-Hedwigs-Kathedrale (St Hedwig's Cathedral)

Mon-Sat 1000-1700, Sun 1300-1700. U-Bahn Hausvogteiplatz. Map 7, F7, p255

Also on the south side of Bebelplatz is the cathedral which was built between 1747 and 1778. While Frederick the Great was willing to grant Roman Catholics a church in the town centre, he was not prepared to pay for it, so it got built as their community could afford to do so. Knobelsdorff modelled it on the Pantheon in Rome. It was rebuilt in 1952, a remarkably early date for the East German Government to restore a religious building. This was probably out of respect for its last priest, Bernhard Lichtenberg, who courageously fought the Nazis and was to die soon after his arrest en route to Dachau Concentration Camp.

Friedrichswerdersche Kirche (Schinkel Museum)

Werderscher Markt. *Tue-Sun 1000-1800. €3. U-Bahn Hausvogteiplatz. Map 7, F7, p255*

This is no longer a church but is now the Schinkel Museum with many of the architect's original drawings. Being a totally gothic, brick structure, it is hard to believe it is the work of Schinkel until one realizes he built it after a visit to England. A collection of 19th-century sculpture is also housed here and several of the artists, notably Johann Gottfried Schadow, were friends of Schinkel.

Frederick the Great on horseback

Unter den Linden/Bebelplatz. *U-Bahn Französische Str. Map 7, E6, p254*

It took a team of sculptors 10 years in the mid-19th century to produce a design the royal family would accept and then to cast it in bronze. For many years after the war, the statue was banished to Potsdam, but as the East German Government became more reconciled to Prussian history the statue was returned here in 1980.

Humboldt-Universität

Unter den Linden 6. *U-Bahn Französische Str. Map 7, E6, p254*

The university was originally built as a palace for Prince Heinrich, the brother of Frederick the Great, but was never used as a royal residence. It was opened as the university in 1810. On the left-hand side of the entrance is the statue of its founder, Wilhelm von Humboldt. The plinth illustrates his interests as an archaeologist, linguist and philosopher. The statute on the right is of his perhaps more famous brother Alexander who was a botanist and explorer. Again his work is brought to life on the plinth. Both marble statues date from 1880. During the week, visitors sometimes join students in their cafeteria as there is little other provision for refreshment

Berlin's monumental architect

Nobody in London coined an adjective "Wrenish", but such was the influence of Karl Friedrich Schinkel (1781-1841) on the architecture of Berlin, that the term "schinkelisch" still exists. Yet Schinkel did not break away from earlier styles as his Bauhaus successors would do a century later. He simply travelled around Europe, sketching, writing and absorbing. He was as overwhelmed by Manchester as he was by Rome. Dudley, in the British Midlands, was however dismissed in one sentence: "It is a town of obelisks, most of which emit smoke." Equally, near home, he would absorb the Gothic of Prussia and the rococo of Bavaria. In Berlin he aimed to emulate the best of what he saw, but he did not want to innovate.

Schinkel was driven to architecture by fire; in 1787 at the age of six he was just old enough to understand and to remember the fire that had destroyed his home town of Neuruppen, northwest of Berlin.

Thirty years later in 1817 the Schauspielhaus (Playhouse) burnt down and Schinkel had to ensure its replacement would be fire-proof. Much of central Berlin would be destroyed by fire bombs between 1943 and 1944. However, the Schinkel buildings survived better than any others. His visits to Britain showed him how iron, just as much as brick and stone, could ensure stability.

Even in the 21st century, Mitte remains a monument to what he created in the early 19th century. Churches, museums, opera houses and gardens have all been maintained or restored to the condition in which he left them.

No amount of traffic and no amount of distant skyscrapers will detract from his legacy. If Berlin ever wanted another name, Schinkelstadt would be the most appropriate.

nearby. At weekends second-hand booksellers set up stands on the pavement by the main entrance to dispose of the works of former academics here who became discredited after 1989.

Museum für Kommunikation (Communication Museum)
Leipzigerstr., www.museumsstiftung.de *Tue-Fri 0900-1700, Sat-Sun 1100-1900. U-Bahn Stadtmitte. Map 6, B8, p253*

This building was founded in 1872 as the first post museum. It adapted in the 1990s to the increasing irrelevance of post and the greater importance of electronic transmission, but was one of the last to integrate with its former opposite number in West Berlin, this being only done in 2000. Older visitors will be reminded of childhood with the display of radiograms, built-in television sets and telex machines. Its stamp collection inevitably reflects the complicated political history Berlin has endured but also includes examples of the very rare Blue Mauritius. This is housed in the basement **Schatzkammer** (Treasury). Mobile robots will entertain some children, but may frighten others.

Neue Wache (New Guardhouse) and Zeughaus (Arsenal)
Unter den Linden. *U-Bahn Französische Str. Map 7, E7, p255*

These two buildings have been remarkably well preserved. The New Guardhouse has for nearly 200 years guarded the dead rather than the living. It was Schinkel's first public building in Berlin. It is worth going inside to see the bronze statue (Mother with her dead son) by Käthe Kollwitz who lost her son in the First World War and her grandson in the Second World War. She just missed enjoying the peace for which she had struggled all her life as she died on 22 April 1945. The surrounding interior just pre-dates the Nazi era, having been completed in 1931. The tombs and the flame are from after the Second World War; one tomb is for the unknown soldier and the other for the unknown concentration camp victim.

The Arsenal is due to reopen as the **Deutsche Historische Museum** (German History Museum) in May 2003. It is hard to believe that for 200 years from its opening in 1695 such an ornate baroque building could be used just for storing arms. Because of this role it was stormed during the 1848 uprisings. It was then briefly a museum before becoming a ceremonial hall towards the end of the 19th century. In East German times it became the German History Museum and with very changed contents it will soon return to this role. Chinese-born architect I.M. Pei was commissioned to build a new glass roof, based on his pyramid designs for the Louvre in Paris.

Schlossplatz (Palace Square)
U-Bahn Hausvogteiplatz. Map 7, F8, p255

This name reflects a hope and a government promise rather than a view offered to a current visitor. Perhaps it would have been better if it had kept its East German name Marx-Engels Platz a little longer. Crossing the River Spree eastwards from Unter den Linden on Schinkel's Schlossbrücke (Palace Bridge), a view emerges of desolation to the right and of vigorous renewal to the left. The desolation results from the destruction of the former **Stadtschloss** (Royal Palace), not so much by bombs from the Second World War, as by a deliberate policy of the East German Government in autumn 1950. At that time Prussian regal history had to be removed from central Berlin so that Moscow-style march-pasts could be arranged in the town centre. The palace had a history of 400 years and was on the scale of those in Potsdam and Charlottenburg with each ruler adding to it. Neither the post-First World War Weimar Republic nor the Nazis had used it for government and in fact it became a mixture of galleries and

! Another Nazi bunker was discovered in 2001. As with the Führerbunker, it was sealed and its location unmarked.

Heavenly heights
Berlin's pleasure gardens, the Lustgarten, as viewed from
the top of Berlin's cathedral

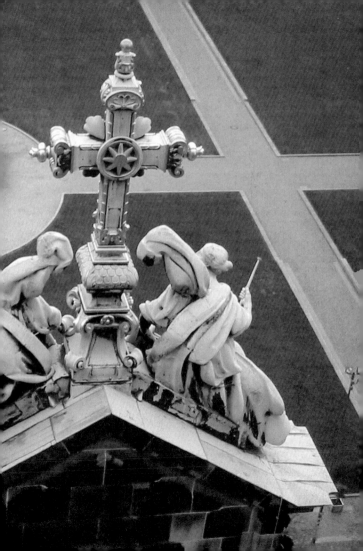

offices. It was used in this way from 1945, so the destruction in 1950 had no rational basis, and this was privately admitted towards the end of the East German era. In 2002, despite acute financial problems, the German Government announced it would rebuild the palace, although no use was specified for the interior.

A different sort of palace was built in its place, one doomed to a much shorter life, however. The **Palast der Republik** built between 1973 and 1976 is due for complete destruction in early 2003, given the danger posed by the asbestos used in its construction. It was given many nicknames, including "Ballast of the Republic" because of its cost and "Eric's Lamp Shop" to ridicule both the number of lights used in it and Erich Honecker, the East German leader at the time. Officially it was "a congress centre, a home for socialist culture, an environment of fun and relaxation for working people and their overseas guests". Many former East Germans now miss it. The catering was good, the shows varied and there were no queues. If many East Germans were cynical about the politics of the place, they were happy it included a bowling alley. Some may have enjoyed the fact that a striptease club had a short lease there in 1990 just as the East German parliament was winding up.

Berliner Dom (Berlin Cathedral)
Karl Liebknecht Str. *Mon-Sat 0900-2000, Sun 1200-2000.*
S-Bahn Hackescher Markt. Map 7, E8, p255

Normally the main cathedral is a high point of any visit to a capital. In Berlin, however, it is impossible to find any admirers for this building. Perhaps, as with the Palace of Culture in Warsaw, it is best to climb to the top, so that the building itself can be ignored. What had originally been a modest construction was torn down and replaced by Kaiser Wilhelm II at the turn of the last century.

It flaunts the arrogance of the time in its use of gold and marble. Apart from the copper dome, good taste gives way to crude opulence. Ironically the brief to the architect was to rival St Peter's in Rome and St Paul's in London. It is thought that when the Royal Palace was blown up, Walter Ulbricht, the East German leader in 1950, wanted to do the same to the cathedral. He is reported to have said that while he could fight art historians, he could not take on the church. It was therefore neglected rather than destroyed. From the 1970s the East German Government was quite happy to take money from West German Protestants to pay for the restoration. The Kaiser though was to have the last laugh. A memorial service was held here for his grandson in October 1994.

Lustgarten (Pleasure Gardens)
S-Bahn Hackescher Markt. Map 7, E8, p255

These now live up to their name. Grass and flowers finally returned in 1998 to reflect the gentler, modern Germany. Military regimes cleared this area for army parades and, not surprisingly, Friedrich Wilhelm I (the soldier king) was the first one to do so in the early 18th century. The first potatoes in Germany were grown here as a delicacy for the royal family. The gardens would later enjoy another "flowering" in the mid-19th century when Peter Joseph Lenné laid out what little land Schinkel had left after the completion of the museums. The Nazis were of course quick to return it to military use and the East Germans ignored the area.

★ Museumsinsel (Museum Island)
www.smb.spk-berlin.de Tue-Sun 1000-1800, Thu till 2200. €6 but free the first Sun in the month. The Bode and Neues museums are closed for several years. S-Bahn Hackescher Markt. Map 7, D7, p255

Museum Island (Bode Museum, Neues Museum, Altes Museum, Pergamon Museum, Alte Nationalgalerie) is currently being reshaped. It is appropriate that one museum and a road bear the name of Wilhelm Bode (1848-1929) who brilliantly combined the

Change of address

In Britain, it is only mass murderers who bring about street-name changes. A house filled with corpses quickly needs a new identity, as does its neighbours. Fortunately, this happens very rarely.

In Berlin, successive political regimes have felt the immediate need to stamp their authority by changing a large number of street names.

The Nazis of course had to honour themselves, successful First World War generals, and they had to dishonour Jews and political opponents. Successive regimes in West and East Berlin have felt the need to honour senior politicians after death.

Then from 1989 there was an eagerness, perhaps an over-eagerness, in former East Berlin to remove names clearly linked with the previous regime. Konrad Adenauer, West Germany's first Chancellor, and Ernst Reuter, West Berlin's first mayor, therefore have large traffic junctions named after them. In the East, the first President, Wilhelm Pieck, had his name given to a street previously named after the French province Lorraine, which the Germans had seized in 1871. The name it now has is Torstrasse (Gate Street) which it had in the early 19th century when it led to one of the gates in the old city wall. Neither the current regime nor its communist predecessor wanted to commemorate earlier German warmongering.

Sometimes the outside world provided convenient neutrality so Mark Twain and Vincent van Gogh are both commemorated. By around 2000, a fairly clear policy had been worked out. Communists who died before East Germany was founded could remain honoured. Rosa

role of scholar, administrator and social networker, always for the benefit of his collections rather than for himself. On many

Luxemburg and Karl Liebknecht, murdered in 1919, and Ernst Thälmann, murdered in 1944, therefore still have their street, their square and their park. These three fought and died for their beliefs so still command great respect. Anyone with a subsequent career was banished into oblivion, whether they were presidents or border guards. Ernst Thälmann did, however, lose his U-bahn Station, which is now called Mohrenstrasse or Moors Street after the Africans whom Friedrich I billeted there in the 17th century.

One pre-war communist, however, was made to suffer. Clara Zetkin was thought to be too much of a fire-brand to allow her name to come up from the East to the doorstep of the Reichstag, an institution she bitterly attacked in the 1920s, although a member of it. Her detractors point to the contempt the communists showed towards parliament in the early 1930s and feel that Nazism might have been defeated had they fought less in the streets and more in parliament. "Her" street has therefore reverted to Dorotheenstrasse, in honour of the wife of Friedrich Wilhelm I. Having lived and died in the 17th century, she can presumably no longer cause offence to anyone. Had Clara Zetkin been commemorated further East in, say, a quiet residential area, it is unlikely her memory would have been disturbed. She was also, dare one say it, "unlucky" to die of natural causes in a Moscow hospital in 1933. Had she lived long enough to have been murdered by the Nazis, her memory would probably have been maintained in the town centre.

occasions he would brief the Kaiser on what to admire when he visited friends. These objects would then always be "given" to the museums. Three words summed up Bode's power "Bode hat gesagt" (Bode has spoken) and a work of art would then be exhibited or condemned to oblivion. A century on, the extent and taste of these collections is still thanks to him.

Altes Museum
Bodestr., Museumsinsel. *Map 7, D8, p255*

The Altes Museum overlooks the Lustgarten and given its design could house only a classical collection. Schinkel called it simply "my best piece of work". As it suffered less than many others during the war, and the Lustgarten has always provided a clear view for the entrance, it is certainly one of his most impressive. An 18-column façade and a Latin inscription 80 m long set the tone. The inscription dedicates the museum to the classics and to liberal arts and notes the year it was built, 1823, and the king on the throne at the time, Friedrich Wilhem III. The collection concentrates on ancient Greece, but goes back to the Etruscans as well. The theme is luxury rather than the day-to-day, with statues, jewellery and ornamental pottery. The life-size 4th-century BC bronze of a boy at prayer and the 1st-century BC silver table service are the major exhibits here. The museum also holds temporary exhibitions on architecture. Designs are always shown too of buildings that were never completed.

Pergamon Museum
Museumsinsel. *Map 7, D7, p255*

The Pergamon Museum does not exhibit mere objects, but whole complexes and streets which surround and absorb the visitor. Its cramped entrance gives no hint of what is to follow: the Pergamon Altar and the Babylonian Street. Both needed some, but not much, reconstruction when they were brought to Germany. The evening lighting is particularly dramatic, the performances of son et lumière even more so. The altar dates from the 2nd century BC and was excavated in the 1870s over an eight-year period in Turkey. It is the largest monument from ancient Greece to have been removed from its original site. The Turks have of course on many occasions requested its return. Do not just look at it from a distance; the intricate friezes of battles between gods and giants demand equal attention. Their message is clear; gods are stable and immortal, whereas humans, however large, are very much the opposite. The blue-tiled processional Babylonian Street is even earlier, dating from the reign of Nebuchadnezzar II in the 6th century BC. Somehow, all the other exhibits in the Pergamon pale into insignificance beside these two, even the remains of the Mshatta City Wall, excavated near Amman. This was actually not looted but was a gift from the Turkish Emperor in 1903.

Alte Nationalgalerie
Bodestr., Museuminsel. *Map 7, D8, p255*

The Alte National Gallery, old to distinguish it from the Neue. (The new one in the Kulturforum near the Potsdamer Platz was founded in 1866, five years before the German nation actually existed.) The collection of 250 paintings was initially a private one. Brought together by the banker Joachim Wagener and by taking this name, art was hopefully going to precede politics. (Prussia imposed its authority on the whole of Germany and on Alsace-Lorraine in 1871 after its defeat of the French.) The museum was in fact conveniently completed in 1871 and the inscription above the entrance, *Der deutschen Kunst* (To German Art), actually gives this year.

Most of Berlin's 19th-century art is now finally displayed together in a single building. One room is devoted to Schinkel's paintings, appropriate as his art has been so little known, and

! Kaiser Wilhelm II abdicated from the Stadtschloss in 1918 but
● was allowed to take 80 trucks of luggage with him into exile.

▶ Past, present and future

Just when Germany is adopting many short sharp sound-bites from English, Berlin has been obsessed by "Vergangenheits-bewältigung", an eight-syllable word literally meaning "overcoming the past". During the 40 years of division, neither side felt particularly eager to assess the Nazi period or the early years of the Cold War. From 1990 onwards, there has been a rush to make amends.

Those old enough to have been active in the Nazi era no longer feel a need to conceal their beliefs and behaviour at that time. In 2002, Traudl Junge, Hitler's last secretary, was happy to publish her memoirs (see also p228) and former soldiers on the Russian front felt no embarrassment in talking on television programmes about their callous treatment of the local people.

The spying activities of the occupying powers can now be openly admitted. The Jewish community has become strong enough again to demand proper and permanent recognition in the form of memorials, museums and restored synagogues. All senior functionaries from East Germany, still alive after reunification, immediately went into print, usually to blame former colleagues for all that went wrong. It is also finally acceptable to express sympathy for the suffering of the Berlin population during years of British bombing.

Berlin has seen quarrels over everything since reunification, but this is a positive sign.

In the 21st century it has elected a homosexual mayor, opened a Jewish museum, adopted the euro and started sightseeing tours with guides stripping as they comment on the sights. Probably the only topic of agreement was the future of Hitler's bunker. It was sealed to prevent it becoming a neo-Nazi shrine. The past in Berlin should soon play the role it does in other capitals, that of a lesson but not of an obsession.

one to Caspar David Friedrich, probably the most famous German artist of this period. Schinkel draws and paints buildings that appeal to him and also shows his designs for future work transposed onto their surroundings. Friedrich, in contrast, shows natural landscapes, usually in bleak winter surroundings. If buildings intrude at all, they are largely abbey ruins. A wonderful enhancement to the collection is the room devoted to French Impressionists.

Nikolaiviertel (St Nicholas Quarter)
S-Bahn and U-Bahn Alexanderplatz. Map 7, F10, p255

With each passing year, critics are slightly less harsh about this area. They, like the buildings, are beginning to mellow and now grant it some atmosphere. When first assembled in 1987, the Nikolaiviertel was simply a film set and a political statement; pseudo-historic was the only formal description it could be given. The East German Government was by then happy to look back on certain aspects of German history and, cynics would say, to cash in on Berlin's 750th anniversary that year. A brand new old town was therefore quickly created near to the sights that tourists always covered. This had been an area badly damaged during the war, damaged in fact with particular relish by the British Royal Air Force in early 1944. They wanted it to be seen as a "final lesson for the German people". It contained no military or industrial targets.

If the quarter is hardly an area for walks, specific buildings and specific restaurants are definitely worth a visit. Some original buildings remain. The **St Nicholas Kirche** is the oldest in Berlin, with a few fragments dating from its foundation in the 14th century. In 1539 it adopted the Reformation. Inside is a small museum detailing Berlin's history until the early 17th century, the most interesting item being a model of the city in the 16th century. The church has three modern organs so is often used for concerts. The **Knoblauchhaus** at Poststrasse 23 commemorates a family that spent 170 years in the house from 1760 and whose members spanned every prestigious field of human activity. The most famous was the architect Eduard (1801-1865) who designed Berlin's largest synagogue on Oranienburgerstrasse. Some of the furniture displayed in the house belonged to him. The **Ephraim-Palais** at Poststrasse 16 is named after Frederick the Great's jeweller and treasurer Veital Heine Ephraim (1703-1775) who financed the Seven Years' War for him, largely by debasing the coinage. So many rogue coins were produced that they became known as "Ephraimites". The building caused the Nazis great problems as Ephraim was Jewish but Frederick was a hero of Hitler's. The compromise reached was to tear down the building but to keep the façade. This baroque façade (divided into 2,500 units) ended up in West Berlin but was returned for the palace to be rebuilt by 1987. The building is now used for temporary exhibitions, usually with 19th-and 20th-century Berlin as the theme. (Listed at www.ephraim-palais.de but only in German.)

Alexanderplatz
U-Bahn and S-Bahn Alexanderplatz. Map 7, C12, p255

Always just "Alex" to the local population, this square has, in an architectural sense, now stood still for over 30 years; hence its interest as a legacy from its role as the centre of East Berlin. In the early 1970s the best that the town could offer was here – its newest hotel, its best-stocked department store and a bookstore with the greatest diversity of reading material that the censors would allow. The square had been widened greatly into the vast pedestrian precinct, which also still remains. The Television Tower nearby (see p62) completed the image of a modern town centre able to look Warsaw and Minsk in the face. Just two office buildings beside the station, the work of Peter Behrens (1868-1940), have survived from earlier times. At ground level, the **Weltzeituhr** (World Clock) has always been a convenient meeting point and when built in 1969 was seen by opponents of the regime as a cruel indication of all the places they were not allowed to visit. Its enamel and aluminium now make it a period piece. The same applies to the fountain next to it, built in much the same way and which has kept its cumbersome old title, the **Brunnen der Völkerfreundschaft** (Fountain of international friendship).

Perhaps because "Alex" was so strongly entrenched amongst Berliners, the square kept its name through both world wars, even though it results from a visit Tsar Alexander I paid to Berlin early in the 19th century. Demonstrations here were often the prelude to changes in regime. The Nazis and communists fought here in the early 1930s and on 4 November 1989 500,000 people demonstrated against the East German Government, just days before the Wall came down. This was totally peaceful; in the 1950s the government built a network of underground tunnels to move police from one side to the other in order to control demonstrations. It was never necessary and they remained unused.

Rotes Rathaus (Red Town Hall)
Alexanderplatz. *S-Bahn and U-Bahn Alexanderplatz. Map 7, E11, p255*

The Red Town Hall (1861-69) did house the municipality in East German times but now, as before 1933, the political composition of the town council is very broadly based. Given the importance of the former royal palace, it is surprising the town hall tower of around 100 m was allowed to be higher than the dome of the palace. However, it is the "stone chronicle", the surrounding 200 m-frieze, that makes this building special. It depicts the history of the city, concentrating on its artists and scientists. In front of the town hall is the much-larger-than-life bronze statue of Karl Marx seated and Friedrich Engels standing to attention beside him. The statue and its accompanying murals and texts turned out to be the final "policy statement" of the East German regime as they were unveiled in 1986, three years before its collapse.

Fernsehturm (Television Tower)

Alexanderplatz, www.berlinerfernsehturm.de *Daily 0900-0100. €6 (€3 for children up to and including 16). No wheelchair access. S-Bahn and U-Bahn Alexanderplatz. Map 7, D11, p255*

When the tower was built in 1969, the East German Government wanted to impress but not offend the USSR. As a result, although 365 m high, this tower was still shorter than the television tower in Moscow. The circular restaurant and the viewing platform are at around 200 m high. Cynics dubbed it "the Pope's revenge" as it was the nearest to a crucifix that contemporary architecture was likely to produce. Others pointed out it was the only view of West Berlin that most easterners would ever get to see. In those days the restaurant used to take an hour to revolve but its capitalist owners have speeded this up to 30 minutes, with the aim of serving twice the number of people in the same amount of time. With illuminations now being so extensive and so powerful all over Berlin, an evening visit is just as enjoyable as a day one.

(Stasi Museum)

Normannstr., www.stasimuseum.de *Tue-Fri 1100-1800, Sat-Sun 1400-1800. €2. U-Bahn Magdalenenstr. Map 1*

The Stasi were the East German secret police, except that they were hardly secret being so pervasive and so numerous. Perhaps their only attempt to keep out of the limelight was the location of this building in Lichtenberg, an otherwise anonymous suburb to the east of Mitte.

The exhibition shows how its 30,000 staff bugged phones, opened letters, noted personal and political indiscretions, all without the help of a single computer. The paperwork was therefore so voluminous that it could not all be destroyed as East Germany came to an end. Plenty is left here as a chronicle to their failure, and they were totally helpless as anti-government

Competitive communism
Flying up the steps to the sky-piercing Television Tower - built by the East Germans in homage to the Russian mother country.

demonstrations spread across the country in 1989. At the head of the organization stood, or rather more usually sat, Erich Mielke. His ultra-bland office has been left entirely as he knew it, a deliberately simple environment to ensure nobody could accuse *him* of succumbing to decadent bourgeois taste.

Tiergarten

*This is undoubtedly Berlin's most changing area. The **Reichstag** (Parliament) used to stand out in bleak isolation. It is now one of many government buildings along the Spree River. The Wall had made the **Potsdamer Platz** equally desolate; it is now almost a town in its own right, a new Manhattan of skyscrapers, cinemas and ethnically diverse cafés. Many governments are ensuring their Tiergarten embassies become true architectural advertisements.*

*Zoo Station used to be where East meets West; the **Lehrter Bahnhof**
is now being converted from a backwater to a new central station for
the whole city. North will meet south here too.*

*Tiergarten means "animal garden" and the second half of the name
is still very appropriate. No amount of pressure from developers has
reduced the wide area of lakes, woods and paths that is such a soothing
antidote in the town centre. You can even pick mushrooms here. Two
reminders of military history, the **Siegesäule** (German Victory
Column) from 1871 and the **Sowjetisches Ehrenmal** (Soviet War
Memorial) from 1945, are also here.*

▸▸ *See Sleeping p128, Eating and drinking p149*

Sights

★ Reichstag (Parliament)

Ebertstr. *Daily 0800-2400. Free, last admission 2200. S-Bahn Unter
den Linden. Map 7, E1, p254*

One of the happiest results of reunification must be the return of
the German Parliament to this building. Its destruction by fire in
February 1933 provided the new Nazi regime with an instant
excuse for dissolving it, so for the next 70 years, it lacked a role. Its
use to house the exhibition "Questions on German History" was
hardly worthy, and the occasional meeting of the West German
Bundestag here was unnecessarily provocative to the East
Germans just a few metres away across the border. Inside, the
building bears no relation to the various interiors it has had since
opening in 1894. This opening had followed 22 years of argument
on the size, layout and location of the building which Germany
clearly needed after its unification in 1871, although the Kaiser was
never keen on such a strong commitment to democracy so close to
his palace. The inscription across the front – "Dem Deutschen Volk"
– (to the German people) was only added in 1916. The exterior has

★ Foster's flight of fancy

Norman Foster's glass dome topping the German Parliament affords panoramic views across central Berlin.

been restored to much as it was, but Norman Foster's new glass dome adds a very late 20th-century look to it, quite apart from the solar heating which it incorporates. Some Russian graffiti from May 1945 has been left. A lift provides quick access to the dome, once in the building, but queues can be very long in the summer during the day. Early morning and evening are good times for avoiding the queues and some visitors have been known to use the separate restaurant entrance at busy times to jump the queue. However access is obtained, the view makes it well worthwhile. Look down on the government area still being built, across to the rising Lehrter Bahnhof which will be Berlin's central station, and up to the skyscrapers that dominate the new Potsdamer Platz.

The surrounding government buildings are called **Das Band des Bundes** (The Ribbon of Government). They are all new and have been deliberately constructed across the Spree River to signify the unity across what had been the border between West and East. These buildings literally show open government. Only the toilets offer glass-free privacy. Otherwise it is possible to look into every office and every meeting hall.

Siegesäule (Victory Column)
Strasse des 17. Juni. *Mon-Thu 0930-1830, Fri-Sun 0930-1930. €1.20. S-Bahn Bellevue. Try to reach the column through the pedestrian tunnels. Leaping in front of the speeding cars is not recommended.* Map 4, B6, p250

In considering all the defeats Germany suffered in the 20th century, it is easy to forget the victories of the 19th. Three in fact occurred within 10 years of each other, against Denmark, Austria and France. This column from 1873 commemorates them. The statues on the north side of the roundabout commemorate the three people most responsible for these victories: Count von Bismarck, who would become Chancellor in 1871, and the two generals von Moltke and von Roon. Von Moltke defeated the

French in the brief but savage 1870-71 war after which Germany seized Alsace and Lorraine as victory spoils. Von Roon was Chief of Staff and then Minister of Defence during these successful military campaigns. In 1938, the Nazis moved the column from in front of the Reichstag to its current location. It is possible to climb the 285 steps to the top and join the Goddess of Victory in looking down, in a sense to the city, but in fact over acres of green as the monument is situated in the middle of the Tiergarten.

One Nazi legacy can also be seen – now the Strasse des 17. Juni which stretches from the Brandenburg Gate to Ernst Reuter Platz, but widened before the war to be the East–West axis of a future "Germania".

● *Photographers should take advantage in winter of the late opening for night-time traffic shots on the roads through the Tiergarten.*

Hamburger Bahnhof-Museum für Gegenwart (Hamburg Station-Museum for the Present)

Invalidenstr. 50. *Tue-Fri 1100-1800, Sat and Sun 1000-1800. €6. S-Bahn Lehrter Bahnhof . Map 2, G1, p246*

Trains stopped running here in the 19th century but the basic station layout has remained. In 1904 rebuilding started on a transport museum which was its role until 1939. The division of the city found it right on the border on the Western side, but owned by the East as it was still nominally a station in the hands of the Reichsbahn (German State Railroad Company). The building was therefore abandoned until the late 1980s when it was bought from the East Germans and converted into an exhibition centre. Once the Wall came down, its role could broaden, and much of its collection is on permanent display. Some "works of art" are clearly here because no other gallery dares touch them. Seemingly haphazard blocks of stone, wood or metal sheeting would still cause much offence elsewhere. Andy Warhol is the main foreign artist displayed and Joseph Beuys the main German one. One piece called *Directional Forces* uses 100 school blackboards, another called *The End of the 20th Century* uses 21 basalt stelae.

Potsdamer Platz
U-Bahn and S-Bahn Potsdamer Platz. Map 6, B5, p253

This complex is almost a town in its own right. Passing through the glass tower blocks which surround it, one does not expect a hint of Italy, but that is what has been created in the centre, at ground level at least. The Renaissance sense of design, the arcades, the ochre tiles and the pastel façades provide a leisurely respite to contrast with the frantic pace of life in the towering Sony Center and the Debis Haus, where any new and successful German company likes to be housed. It would be easy to spend a whole holiday around the platz; there is ample greenery and water during the good weather and ample culture for the greyer days. Casinos and night clubs are also as prominent here as in their traditional locations near to Zoo Station.

Before the war the Nazis began to pull down some buildings to prepare for a new north–south axis. Between 1945 and 1961 it was a centre for several political dramas whilst the border stayed open; the most violent day was 17 June 1953 when Westerners had to watch strikes being crushed by Russian tanks. After 1961, on the Western side there were no capitalist grounds for building so close to the border, cut off from potential customers and employees. On the Eastern side the area was in the "death strip" so all buildings had to be cleared. Only an empty space was needed for border patrols in the watchtowers to look down on. From the West, tourists came to gawp across the Wall, but the local population was by and large too sad to do so.

Suddenly in 1990 the area became instantly desirable. By 2000 everything above ground was complete. (Underground was a very different matter. Financial cutbacks from 2001 have stalled the

Remains of the day
A child leans against a remnant of the Berlin Wall that marks the former East-West divide in Potsdamer Platz.

completion of both a north–south railway and road link.) Its international air has been assured by the range of architects involved in the planning – Renzo Piano from Italy, Richard Rogers from London, the German Hans Kollhoff and the German-American Helmut Jahn. By naming the main square after Marlene Dietrich, a singer was chosen who was liked just as much abroad as in Germany. Appropriately the **Filmmuseum Berlin** is here (Tuesday-Wednesday, Friday-Sunday 1000-1800, Thursday 1000-2000) and nothing is concealed. The Nazi era is covered as extensively as the 1920s, before moving on to the bitter East/West divide after the war. Leni Riefenstahl celebrated her 100th birthday in 2002 and has a whole room devoted to her highly controversial career as a film director.

History is also not completely forgotten in the **Sony Center**. It houses the **Kaisersaal** (Emperor's Room) from the former Grand Hotel Esplanade which was on this site. This small section of the building actually survived both the war and the Wall, although retaining its former glamour was out of the question.

Erotik Museum (Erotic Museum)

Joachimstalerstr. 4. *Daily 0900-2400. €5 Admission only to those of 18 or over. U-Bahn and S-Bahn Zoo. Map 4, D3, p250*

There are plenty of perfectly innocent silk paintings here from China and Japan, together with miniature statues from Africa. There are drawings by the very respectable Heinrich Zille and there is also a room devoted to the very open studies carried out by the homosexual scientist Magnus Hirschfeld until he had to flee to Nice in 1933, when his library provided the basis for the Burning of the Books in Opera Square, see p43. There are also numerous other objects, unsurprisingly, of not such an innocent nature.

Bargains

Best

- City-run museums are free on Wednesdays
- The bookstalls in front of Humboldt-Universität
- A café with the menu written in Turkish and German
- Aldi and Pennymarkt shops

Sowjetisches Ehrenmal (Soviet War Memorial)

Tiergarten. S-Bahn Unter den Linden. Map 4, B10, p251

This was the first new building completed by the Russians in 1945 and was inaugurated on their national day, 7 November. It is a sort of prelude to the much larger memorial that would follow in Treptow several kilometres to the east. This one specifically commemorates the 20,000 Russian soldiers who died in the Berlin area of whom around 2,500 are buried on this site. The marble used was taken from Hitler's chancellery building and the tanks that are beside the column were those that first reached the nearby Reichstag. Being just inside West Berlin, shifts of Russian soldiers used to be brought for a regular changing of the guard. They are now less committed to it, but the German Government has agreed to maintain the site, which largely amounts to keeping demonstrators away.

Bauhaus-Archiv (Bauhaus Collection)

Klingelhöferstr. 14, www. bauhaus-archiv.de 1000-1700 except Tue, €7.80. U-Bahn Nollendorfplatz. Map 4, D7, p251

The Bauhaus was the best-known school of art and design during the 1920s. It had a turbulent history from its founding in 1919 in Weimar, through to its move to Dessau, and then to its final year in Berlin before it was closed by the Nazis in 1933. Few of its major participants got on with each other and they did not attempt to keep the school going in exile in the USA. Its slogan was "Art and Technology, a new unity" and it aimed to show that good taste and mass production were not incompatible. It would, however, retain a continuing worldwide influence which encouraged the West Berlin authorities to commemorate its work with this building. The founder of this building was the architect Walter Gropius (1883-1969) and he provided the initial conception for housing the collection but it was only completed in 1979, 10 years after his death. What is shown changes regularly, but there is always a selection of designs for actual buildings and for the many that stayed on the drawing board. It is often forgotten that the Bauhaus, like Jugendstil 30 years earlier, influenced interiors just as much as exteriors so this exhibition also covers furniture, pottery and metalwork.

Prenzlauerberg

To those who knew the area at all before the Wall came down, it meant dissent, an unusual commodity in East Germany, even when the Soviet Union had embraced perestroika. Perhaps it suited the regime to ignore much of what went on here, taking comfort from the fact that risqué behaviour did not spread out until near the end of the regime in summer 1989.

In fact the 750th anniversary of Berlin in 1987 was used as a pretext for bringing back some streets to 1900 with gas lamps and water pumps. The past seemed safer than the future to show both residents and visitors. Nobody need rebel now and the area is one largely devoted to pleasure. It is, however, locals who enjoy themselves here; foreigners so used to speaking English in the city centre now have to turn to their broken German. Enjoyment is possible during the day, but is at its best at night.

*Reminders of harsher times are the **Jewish Cemetery**, the statue of **Käthe Kollwitz** and several local museums and galleries. On a happier note, visit the **Vitra Design Museum** which shows what Germans liked and did not like for their houses over the last few decades. The brick wall exterior is uninviting; everything inside certainly isn't.*

▸ *See Sleeping p128, Eating and drinking p150, Bars and clubs p166*

Sights

Gedenkstätte Berliner Mauer (Berlin Wall Memorial)
Bernauerstr. *S-Bahn Nordbahnhof. Map 2, E4, p246*

What, if anything, of the Berlin Wall should be maintained was an immediate subject of dispute as the souvenir hunters started to hack pieces off in November 1989. Architecturally, it hardly deserved a preservation order, and historically it could only bring back sad memories. The final compromise was to leave just a very few segments in their original location. The Bernauerstrasse was linked with all cross-border activities. As houses on one side of the street were in the East and the street itself was in the West, it became in August 1961 the scene of desperate leaps from tenement windows before they were bricked up and the tenants moved out. The longest-lasting escape tunnel went under this street and on 9 November 1989, it was the first border post to be opened to the throng of East Germans demanding to be let through.

During 2002 part of the former Wall was rebuilt so that it now looks as it did when it was in use. In 2003 a large museum will open giving full background to all the dramas here between 1961 and 1989. The Church of Reconciliation, which found itself in the death strip, was blown up by the East Germans in 1985, but a new chapel has been built on the site to replace it.

Street life
Passing the time of day around Hackesche Markt.

Hackesche Höfe
www.hackesche-hoefe.com *S-Bahn Hackescher Markt.*
Map 7, B9, p255

Eight linked courtyards of residential accommodation were built
here in 1906. They were ahead of their time in many ways.
Working-class people for the first time enjoyed central heating,
inside toilets and balconies. They also enjoyed the Jugendstil
colourfully glazed tiling and the long, deep windows of the famous
architect August Endell. They descended staircases decorated with
patterns based on leaves and flowers. Communities were mixed,
and on the ground floor, businesses were equally varied, the idea
being that the successful should support the failures. Who would

know when roles might be reversed? The slump in the 1930s hit the courtyards as it did the rest of Berlin, and despite several individual acts of supreme bravery, the large Jewish community was gradually eliminated by the Nazi round-ups.

Little was done to restore the area after the war but 1987, the 750th anniversary of the founding of Berlin, gave East Germany a pretext to show what excellent architecture it was capable of producing. The work continued after reunification and the cross-section of inhabitants and businesses must now be very similar to what it was before the First World War. Only the restaurants are different; they have an international menu and an international clientele. Go on a sunny day and sit outside. Service may well be slow but with storey after storey of Jugendstil, this hardly matters.

To see streets that now bear no relation to their past, walk through the courtyards to Sophienstrasse and Auguststrasse, where smart clothes shops and art galleries have displaced their mundane predecessors. Here West and East are now meaningless terms; there is nowhere else in Berlin for career-minded young designers and painters to be seen. Only when they pass 40 can they risk a move elsewhere.

● *Before leaving the area, take a peep at the two gardens in Auguststrasse 69, one a seasonal one and one an artistic one, with the flowers as a backdrop to sculpture.*

Neue Synagoge (New Synagogue)
Oranienburgerstr. 28-30, www.cjudaicum.de   *Sun-Thu 1000-1800, Fri 1000-1400. S-Bahn Oranienburger Str. Map 7, B6, p254*

Eduard Knoblauch sadly did not live to see the completion of his masterpiece in 1866, which he had modelled on the Alhambra in Granada, Spain. However, he left it in good hands, with August Stüler ensuring his standards would be maintained. Both Chancellor Bismarck and members of the royal family attended the consecration to stress their support for the Jewish community. It was the largest synagogue in Germany, seating over 3,000 people, and the central cupola with its gilded ribbing is 46 m high. It was successfully defended from SS attacks on Kristallnacht in 1938 when most other Berlin synagogues were destroyed, but was badly bombed in 1943. Rebuilding started at the end of East German times and it was reconsecrated in 1988, although with a much smaller hall as the remains of the original one had been removed in 1958. Perhaps with a feeling of guilt, the East German leader Erich Honecker attended the opening in 1988, but unusually for him at a public event, he did not speak.

Kollwitz Denkmal (Kollwitz Memorial)
Kollwitz Platz. *U-Bahn Senefelder-Platz.* *Map 2, E8, p247*

Käthe Kollwitz was described in East German times simply as the "great proletarian artist" as she lived in this area from 1891 to 1943 and most of her work, both on canvas and in stone, projects poverty and the tragedy of war. She lost a son in the First World War and a grandson in the Second World War and died just before the end of the war in April 1945. This statue of her was completed in 1958. The one of the mother clutching her son is from a design of hers but was completed in 1951 (see p48). The garden surrounding it is the site of her house which was destroyed in a bombing raid in 1943. Ironically the museum of her work is now on one of Berlin's most fashionable streets in Charlottenburg to the west, see p82. Her husband was a doctor to the poor of this area.

Jüdischer Friedhof (Jewish Cemetery)
Schönhauser Allee. *U-Bahn Senefelder-Platz.* *Map 2, E8, p247*

This dates from 1828 when it was situated well outside the city. Any prominent Jew who died in the 19th century would be buried here. From 1880 onwards burials were restricted to families already with a plot. The most famous funeral to take place here was of the painter Max Liebermann in 1935, who had lived most of his life on the Pariser Platz, beside the Brandenburg Gate. Attendance by non-Jews was minimal, given the dangers they would face being seen to have associated with such a famous Jew. The artist Käthe Kollwitz took the risk and none of her works were subsequently exhibited in Germany. The cemetery was surprisingly not plundered by the Nazis until early 1945. It was somewhat neglected in East German times. There is now a gradual programme of renovation and documentation underway.

Vitra Design Museum

Kopenhagenerstr. 58, www.design-museum-berlin.de
Tue-Sun 1100-2000, Fri late opening till 2200. €5.50.
U-Bahn and S-Bahn Schönhauser Allee. Map 2, B7, p247

This museum of high brick walls was once an electricity transformer station. What surprises visitors is the use to which the former interior has been put. The one large display area, 100 yards long and 7 yards wide, is also unusual for the arts world. There is no permanent display here, but each exhibition centres on interior design, usually for offices and public buildings. Nothing is neglected. The lighting and the curtains are as important as the desks and the carpets.

Kunstwerke BERLIN (Institute for Contemporary Art)

Auguststr. 69, **T** 243 4590, www.kw-berlin.de *Tue-Sun 1200-1800.*
€4, concessions €2.50, children under 12 years free. S-Bahn Oranienburger Str., U-Bahn Oranienburger Tor. Map 7, A6, p254

This old margarine factory converted into an art house provides four floors for temporary exhibitions. The huge basement has been used as an arena for video installations and film projections. The space has been used by artists as varied as the Wilson sisters in

Making a move
A sculpture adorns the Kulturbraueri, a former brewery turned cultural and music space, Schönhauser Allee, Prenzlauerberg.

their filmic interpretations of Russian spacecraft, to Alejandro Gonzáles Iñárritu, the director of *Amores Perros*, and his collaboration with the Belgian artist Francis Alÿs to explore cut material from the film.

● *Take the slide from the first floor to the intriguing garden of bamboo poles and flowering bean plants, in which sits the Café Bravo and bar of mirrors and perfect angles, designed by the celebrated architect Dan Graham.*

Eigen + Art
Auguststr. 26, **T** 280 66 05, www.eigen-art.com *Tue- Fri 1100-1800, Sat 1200-1800. U-Bahn Oranienburger Tor, S-Bahn Oranienburger Str., U-Bahn Weinmeisterstr. Map 7, A6, p254*

The Leipzig-born owner Gerd Lybke started the gallery in Auguststrasse shortly after the Wall came down. East German artists are promoted here with many of them having taken part in Documenta X, the Kassel-based art festival.

Galerie Bodo Niemann
Auguststr. 19, **T** 49 30 28 39. *Tue-Fri 1300-1800. Map 7, A6, p254*

This is mainly a photographic gallery with maybe the odd original print of Man Ray's. The exhibitions are always fairly small as well as the photos – portraits and lots of black and white. It is sleek and sedate and nice to wander around.

Charlottenburg

Charlottenburg will never reclaim the role it won when Berlin was divided. Then, it was a showcase enjoying massive subsidies from the Bonn government. The aim was always to show West Berlin in contrast to the East so visitors to both would always leave with a positive impression of the West and would always support the Bonn government in pushing for closer integration between West Berlin and the Federal Republic. The Kurfürstendamm was a mile-long advertisement for capitalism; excellence could be taken for granted in every shop. Now it has to compete with Mitte and Prenzlauerberg. However, it still has its name, taken from the **palace**, some of which has survived since 1700. It also has many of the institutions that made West Berlin so famous: the **Gedächtniskirche** (Memorial Church) was on every postcard, as was **KaDeWe**, Berlin's most famous department store, or the Kranzler-Eck, its equally famous café. Only since 1990 can it reveal its underground city, built in readiness for a nuclear attack, and now part of the **Story of Berlin** museum. Side streets are as important as the avenues. Look there for Jugendstil architecture, but equally for glass temples such as the "shrine" to **Ludwig Erhard**, the German Chancellor, credited with the 1960s' economic miracle, see p83.

➤➤ See Sleeping p131, Eating and drinking p155, Bars and clubs p169

 ## Sights

Gedächtniskirche (Memorial Church)

Breitscheidplatz. *Daily 0900-1900 for the church, Mon-Sat 1000-1600 for the exhibition.* S-Bahn and U-Bahn Zoologischer Garten. Map 4, D3, p250

The full name for this church is the Kaiser Wilhelm Gedächtniskirche as it was built shortly after the Kaiser's death in 1888. Only the framework of the tower remained in 1945 and it seemed logical to take it down and rebuild the site from scratch. Discussion raged for years and on one occasion 50,000 people came to demonstrate in favour of keeping what had by then been called the "hollow tooth". Only in 1961 was a plan agreed, with the tower staying and the current single-storey honeycomb being added so that worship could again take place here. The exhibition in the tower was assembled only in 1987; it contains a few remnants from the earlier building, including some mosaics and photographs of the 1943 devastation. The church became what would now be called a logo for West Berlin, a surprising symbol in view of the modern image the town in other respects wanted to create as a contrast to its Eastern neighbour.

Breitscheidplatz
S-Bahn and U-Bahn Zoologischer Garten. Map 4, D4, p250

Breitscheidplatz shows Berlin at its brashest and brightest. Neon lights abound, cafés stay open through most of the night, and by day street markets and shops belie the alleged financial crisis that Berlin is supposed to have suffered since 2000 or so. The Mercedes-Benz star continues to rotate from the 22-storey Europa building. This was constructed in 1965 to impress all visitors and locals with the stability of West Berlin at a time when it felt increasingly threatened from the East. Inside, the casino is one of a hundred outlets for spending money although it is possible to admire for free the fountains playing. Mammon has certainly taken over the Breitscheidplatz from God.

KaDeWe
Tauentzienstr. 21-24, www.kadewe.de Mon-Fri 0930-2000, Sat 0930-1600. U-Bahn Wittenbergplatz. Map 4, E4, p250

Many a learned book has been written on the downfall of East Germany, but probably these three syllables did more damage to the regime than any nuclear threat from the West, or any internal dissident. KaDeWe is the popular abbreviation for Kaufhaus des Westens which has kept its reputation as Berlin's best department store through every change of regime. "West" came to have tremendous political significance during the era of division but the name has always been the same since it was founded in 1907.

Then, as now, the food hall on the top floor is the major draw, not that it actually uses such a down-to-earth name. It is of course the "Feinschmecker Etage" (gourmet floor). The worrying statistics for the East German Government were the 1,000 varieties of wurst (sausage) always available here and the West German media ensured that this was never forgotten "drüben" (over there). Statistics for wine or spices could be written off as being irrelevant to day-to-day life. Wurst appears daily on every German dining table and if capitalism produces it better than socialism, the public would see it as a better system.

KaDeWe has succeeded by not becoming too elitist. Ordinary shoppers, in the best sense of the term, are to be seen there. It mixes Berliners as few other places can do. Being so much part of the establishment, KaDeWe of course also now has a Reichstag-style glass dome, and a restaurant for looking down on the rest of the world. It is hardly necessary to comment on the quality or variety of the food there. Its extensive menus can be checked on the website. See also shopping p193.

Käthe-Kollwitz-Museum
Fasanenstr. 24, www.kaethe-kollwitz.de *Wed-Mon 1100-1800. €5. U-Bahn Uhland Str. Map 4, E2, p250*

It is hard to picture a more inappropriate address than this for an exhibition of the work of Käthe Kollwitz (1867-1945). Fasanen-strasse is the Jermyn Street of Berlin where good taste and affluence have always intermingled. Käthe Kollwitz, however, devoted her life to painting the poor. She wrote in her autobiography: "The bourgeoisie do not appeal to me, whereas the workers affect me deeply." She lived in Prenzlauerberg, at the time one of the most deprived areas of Berlin. The street where she spent 50 years now carries her name. This museum covers all that time and she hammered out a pacifist theme until the end, although the Nazis banned public displays of her work towards

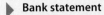

Bank statement

Ludwig Erhard will be a name often mentioned in Berlin over the next few years as the city struggles for the first time since the war with an economic crisis. Erhard was Economics Minister and then Chancellor of West Germany in the early 1960s when his name was closely linked with the "Wirtschaftswunder", the economic miracle, which was simply just that. As Britain and France lurched from one crisis to another, he gave his country prosperity, stability, low unemployment and above all an economy almost free of inflation. Over the Berlin Wall in the East, his legacy would remain an envied and so forbidden fruit.

His name has been given to the building now used by the Berlin Chamber of Commerce and the Berlin Stock Exchange on Fasanenstrasse (see map p4, D2, p250). Designed by British architect Nicholas Grimshaw, the Ludwig Erhard Haus has been nicknamed "The Armadillo", as the design most closely resembles this mammal.

As with the parliamentary buildings, openness is its theme, so glass is the main material used. To see how the economy is faring, look at the faces of the employees; see how many of the offices are occupied, see who arrives by bus and who by car. When the building is again full of smiling faces, Berlin's desperately needed second "Wirtschaftswunder" will have arrived.

the end of her life. She would never relax and sadness pervades all her work. Most of her work was with drawings, not paintings, since the sadness she wished to portray was more effective in that medium. Several works centre on the theme of mothers losing their sons in war – her own died at the front in 1915 – and of mothers too poor to feed their families. See also p48 and p76.

★ Story of Berlin

Kurfürstendamm 207, www.story-of-berlin.de *Daily 1000-2000 with last admission at 1800. €9.30. The whole museum is in English. U-Bahn Uhland Str., S-Bahn Savigny-Platz. Map 4, E1, p250*

To have an indulgent visit, linger in the 19th-century area when most wars that intruded were successful for the Prussians. To be shocked, stay in the 20th-century zone. Several senses are tested here too. No visitor forgets their trample over the charred books avidly burnt in 1933 (see p44) or the smashing glass from Kristall-nacht (when thousands of Jewish synagogues and businesses were destroyed, 100 people died and thousands were arrested) five years later. In a happier mode, they will remember just as clearly the bank of television screens announcing the opening of the Wall in 1989.

The bomb shelter below the building can be visited only on guided tours, which take place on the hour. What a pity they were only built during the Cold War, so were never used, rather than a few years earlier when they could have been fully occupied every night for two years. This one is a complete underground town, totally cut off from the world above to prevent radiation seeping in. The largest room is the hospital, the smallest the armoury.

★ Schloss Charlottenburg (Charlottenburg Palace)

Tue-Sun 1000-1700. The main palace is open year-round, but some of the outer buildings close between 1 Nov and 31 Mar. €7. Admission covers most of the buildings in the grounds, though entry times there can sometimes vary slightly from those of the main palace. U-Bahn Richard-Wagner-Platz or Sophie-Charlotte-Platz. Map 5, D3, p252

This palace needs to be appreciated from a distance just as much as from its grounds. Although the U-Bahn station Sophie-Charlotte-Platz is not the nearest, do not begrudge the kilometre walk or so from there along Schlossstrasse. However good or bad the weather, the baroque cupola will stand out and entice you closer – note the **Goddess of Fortune** on top acting as a weather-vain. This gradual approach is also the best way to take in the 500-yard wide façade. The statue of Friedrich Wilhelm I in the central courtyard has had, even on Berlin standards, a chequered history since the war. Originally located outside the Royal Palace in the East, it was moved to Potsdam for safe-keeping, sunk in a barge on the Tegel Lake in 1946 where it stayed for six years before being brought up and placed here as an alternative to returning it to East Berlin. At the height of the Cold War, the Charlottenburg Palace was the only secure legacy from the 500-year history of the Hohenzollern Prussian royal family.

Queen Charlotte (1669-1705) was the wife of Friedrich I (1657-1713) and the first, relatively small, palace was built as her summer residence. It was expanded after 1701 when Friedrich ceased to be a mere prince and had crowned himself King of Prussia. The palace became a congenial escape for her from her totally incompatible husband. He was boorish and vain, she cultured and modest, and she surrounded herself here with the best and the brightest from the worlds of art and philosophy. She died when she was 36 years old and the original name of the Palace, Lietzowburg, was changed in her memory. Subsequent kings spared just as little expense in enlarging this palace as they did with the Royal Palace in the town centre and with Potsdam. The surrounding area was totally dependent on the use the royal family made of it. When the Hohenzollerns were losing wars, the villagers had to return to agriculture. When wars were won, several hundred congenial jobs would then result here.

The palace can be seen as a one-stop shop for two centuries of German architecture from 1700 to 1900. It mirrors the relationship with France throughout that time. The influence of Versailles is clear, both in the buildings and in the very formal gardens behind them.

Inside, the **Knobelsdorff Flügel** is the section with the most elaborate interior, and the most lavish displays. The **Weisse Saal**

★ Palace Guard
The 17th-century Schloss Charlottenburg with the statue of Friedrich Wilhelm I in the foreground.

(White Hall) was the banqueting and throne room combined. The decoration in the 50-yard long **Golden Gallery**, depicting the four seasons and the four elements, is based on a design by the French artist Antoine Watteau. Frederick the Great was an admirer of his and eight paintings of his are exhibited in the palace. (A wide range of 19th-century German paintings, including those of Caspar David Friedrich, which used to be shown here are now in the Alte Nationalgalerie on Museumsinsel, see p57.)

The **Porzellankabinett** (Porcelain Gallery) concentrates on blue and white designs from both China and Japan. The entire wall, from floor to ceiling is covered with porcelain.

The **Museum für Vor und Frühgeschichte** (Museum of Pre and Early History) is housed in the former palace theatre. Many of the finds stem from excavations needed to build the German motorway system. The high point of the collection is what the famous, or perhaps infamous, Heinrich Schliemann brought back from Troy in the mid-19th century after he first discovered the site. Some of the items are copies as it was assumed the originals had been destroyed in the war, but in the early 1990s they turned up in the cellars of the Pushkin Museum in Moscow.

Outside, in the gardens, a number of buildings should be visited. The **Mausoleum** was built in 1810 after the death of Queen Luise, wife of Friedrich Wilhelm III, and was then extended in 1841 to bury him, and again in 1890 to bury three more members of the family. Architecturally, the building stands out for its classical design, in contrast to the baroque and rococo of the palace.

The **Schinkel Pavilion**, also classical, was modelled specifically on a villa in Naples where Friedrich Wilhelm II had stayed in 1822. Particularly incongruous for Germany are its small square rooms and the outdoor rather than indoor marble furniture placed within them. More appropriate are the drawings and paintings by Schinkel and by several contemporaries of his which are also displayed here.

9 November in German history

Four major events in the 20th-century that have taken place on this day:

1918 Kaiser Wilhelm II abdicated. On 11 November the armistice ended the Second World War.

1923 Hitler launched a failed coup in Munich.

1938 Kristallnacht: Synagogues and Jewish businesses were destroyed.

1989 The Berlin Wall was opened.

The **Belvedere** combines a classical and a baroque façade with neither being overpowering. It is hard to believe it is the work of the same architect who designed the Brandenburg Gate – Carl Gotthard Langhans. Do look to the top of the cupola to see three cherubs holding up a basket of flowers. Officially it was a teahouse but it came to be used more for the royal family's extra-marital affairs. The location of the Belvedere beside the Spree provided a discreet entry and exit point. Now it houses a 19th-century porcelain collection from KPR (Königliche Porzellan-Manufaktur), the company that held the royal warrant. A mere glance at the variety and skill of their work shows why they had no competitors.

Ägyptisches Museum (Egyptian Museum)

Schlossstr. 70. *Tue-Sun 1000-1800. €6, free first Sun in the month. S-Bahn Westend, U-Bahn Richard-Wagner-Platz.*
Map 5, E3, p252

The best articles in this field were in East Berlin during the division so what is here is largely what happened to have been hidden away from the Pergamon towards the end of the war. It is supplemented with some gifts by the Egyptian Government made later in return for the help given by the West Germans in the building of the Aswan Dam. Many visitors come for just one item – the 14th-century BC bust of Queen Nefertiti, and then take a cursory glance at the day-to-day ephemera of ancient Egypt which make up much of the remaining collection.

Sammlung Berggruen (Berggruen Collection)

Schlossstr. 1. *Tue-Fri 1000-1800, Sat-Sun 1100-1800. €6, free first Sun in the month. S-Bahn Westend, U-Bahn Richard-Wagner-Platz. Map 5, E3, p252*

This collection is often now simply known as the Picasso Museum because of the predominance of his works there. However, this is perhaps unfair on the founder Heinz Berggruen (b 1914). He is one of the very few members of the pre-war Jewish refugee community who returned to Berlin; even fewer have been as philanthropic as he has been. He left for America in 1936 with 10 Deutschmarks in his pocket. After the war, he set up a gallery in Paris which is how he came to know Picasso so well. The collection, which opened in 1996 in the former royal barracks, has been sold to the city for much less than the price offered by American museums so is now a permanent feature of the city. About €100,000,000 seems a lot of money but is nothing compared to what Berggruen could have made elsewhere. There are 70 different works of Picasso from all periods of his life. There cannot be many other galleries where paintings by Braque, Cézanne and van Gogh seem almost to be a side show. Even the whole room devoted to Paul Klee cannot approach the breadth of the Picasso collection. It is an ironic end to Berggruen's career that he has returned to found, in what was the Nazi capital, a gallery devoted 100% to *entartete Kunst* (degenerate art), the generic term the Nazis used for any works not in official favour.

Bröhan-Museum

Schlossstr. 1a, **T** 326 906 00, www.broehan-museum.de *Tue-Sun 1000-1800. €4. S-Bahn Westend, U-Bahn Richard-Wagner-Platz. Map 5, E3, p252*

Just in case any visitors arrive with any misapprehensions about the exhibits, the museum is subtitled Museum for Art Nouveau, Art Deco and Functionalism 1889-1939. However, whatever anyone's expectations, few will regret immersing themselves in the best taste from all the applied arts over these 50 years. German industrialist Karl Bröhan only began to assemble this collection in the mid-1960s. For about a decade he showed it privately in his villa but then in 1982 he gave the entire collection of 2,500 items to the city of Berlin. His aim is to show how important artistry can be in all items of day-to-day life. Come here as an antidote to the rococo at the palace; the materials are commonplace in the furniture as much as in the fabrics or in the china; there is not a single item which could not be used on a day-to-day basis but would anyone now dare to do so? 1939 brought functionalism with a very small "f" to the whole of Europe so it is appropriate the collection ends with that year.

★ Kulturforum

Cultural Centre. *Tue-Fri 1000-1800, Sat-Sun 1100-1800. Late night opening on Thu til 2200. €6 for all museums combined. S-Bahn and U-Bahn Potsdamer Platz. Map 6, B2, p253*

With Museumsinsel in East Berlin, West Berlin soon felt the need to have a centre of its own to compete. Inevitably it had to be bigger and more extensive so it would cover music as well as art. Planning started in the 1950s but the building of the Wall in 1961 accelerated the process since for several years afterwards not only were Easterners kept from the West, but Westerners were not allowed into the East. The location was, however, dictated by the

Berlin is not pretty, it is not charming but it is one of the most exciting urban environments and almost, it seems strange to say, Mediterranean in its emotional warmth.

Sir Simon Rattle

politics of the 1950s when the border was still open. The West wanted a cultural inducement as near to the border as it was practical to build. Ironically several of the buildings have a very East German look about them with their use of concrete, chandeliers and pale wood plus the ample space in all the reception areas. The Kulturforum now competes in a sense with the Potsdamer Platz; here is a predictable artistic and musical environment whereas there, anything goes!

Philharmonie
Kulturforum. *See above for opening hours and prices. Tours of the building take place during the day both in English and in German at 1300. Free. Map 6, B3, p253*

The Philharmonie, where Simon Rattle has presided since the summer of 2002, is best known for its circular auditorium with "vineyard" seating that accommodates around 2,200, but where no seat is more than 30 m from the conductor. It is a surprising modern work bearing in mind the architect Hans Scharoun was nearly 70 years old when he completed it in 1963. His background as a town planner in the desperate years immediately after the war comes out in many aspects of the design. There are no intimate corners, no place for nature, and certainly none for luxury. The assumption is clearly that at least 1,000 people will always be inside and will always be a collective. Scharoun has had one street beside the Philharmonie named after him, and the other is named after its most famous conductor, Herbert von Karajan.

Gemäldegalerie (Picture Gallery)
Kulturforum. *See Kulturforum, p90, for opening hours and prices. Map 6, C2, p253*

This gallery is one of the very few to rival the National Gallery in London for the breadth of its collection, but has the space for every single picture to be enjoyed. The gallery will probably be the final addition to the Kulturforum, having been completed in 1998 to house a collection that had been split between the Bode Museum in the East, and the Dahlem Museum in the West. It is an impartial European union, covering the 13th-18th centuries, with paintings by Botticelli, Cranach the Elder, Dürer, Gainsborough and Rembrandt through to Velázquez. There are 30 pictures from Cranach and 16 from Rembrandt. To see the pictures in greater depth, examine them online in the basement computer centre.

Kunstgewerbemuseum (Applied Arts Museum)
Kulturforum. *See p90 for opening hours and prices.* Map 6, B2, p253

Visitors start their visit on the lower ground floor where the most recent acquisitions are housed – a laptop computer from 1999, electric typewriter and radiogram from the 1960s. Middle floors are more conventional with the expected silver goblets, Meissen china, and early crucifixes; however, a trip to the top floor is certainly worthwhile for the Jugendstil designs on the glassware and ceramics. The museum was built for this collection in the early 1980s but provides a rather austere backdrop for it.

Neue Nationalgalerie (Modern Art Gallery)
Kulturforum. *See p90 for opening hours and prices.* Map 6, C2, p253

It is sad that this is the one building Mies van der Rohe designed for post-war Berlin. He claimed he was influenced by Schinkel but to many it resembles an office block he had previously designed for a coal company in Brasilia. As he died soon after it was completed in 1968, he was unable to defend his reputation.

! In 1937 20,000 people a day visited an exhibition of "degenerate" paintings, all by artists whom the Nazis otherwise banned from public exhibition.

Christian reflection
The church of St Matthew's reflected in Mies van der Rohe's glass box (the Neue Nationalgalerie)

Light streams in to the ground floor, but this is only for temporary exhibitions. Late 19th and most of the 20th-century German art has its permanent resting place in the basement, with the newer work all going to Hamburger Bahnhof, p67. The Bauhaus and Brücke movements both have their dedicated museums in Berlin, but a good selection of their work is offered here, together with that of artists such as Oskar Kokoschka and Otto Dix who cannot be placed into a specific school. Much of what should have been here was destroyed by the Nazis as "degenerate"; it was fortunate that many collectors and curators hid away these paintings until after the war.

A few works by non-Germans are displayed and they provide the link with art in a much broader sense of the term at Hamburger Bahnhof. The massive "Who's afraid of Red Yellow and Blue?" by the American painter Barnett Newman provides an appropriate conclusion to this display. Anything more unconventional would not have hung happily with pre-war German masters.

Kreuzberg

*Kreuzberg is hard to typecast; to some it is the former Prenzlauerberg which in the 1980s attracted the young, the artistic and the unconventional. To others it is now the Turkish quarter, reflected in many streets where hardly a German shop sign is to be seen. Yet this ignores Yorkstrasse with some of the most expensive houses in all Berlin. The sights are mainly ones for contemplation and sadness – detailing Nazi crimes at the **Topographie des Terrors** museum and seeing the results of allied bombing in the shell of Anhalter railway station, and the desperate attempts to leave East Germany portrayed at the **Haus am Checkpoint Charlie**. Others, such as the **Jüdisches Museum**, now offer hope. Only the **Deutsches Technikmuseum** offers an escape from politics.*

▸▸ *See Sleeping p136, Eating and drinking p156, Bars and clubs p170*

Sights

Haus am Checkpoint Charlie
Friedrichstr. 43-45, www.mauer-museum.com *Daily 0900-2200.*
€7. U-Bahn Koch Str. Map 6, C8, p253

It used to be sad that a crucial part of Berlin's history was dealt with in such an amateur manner, in cramped noisy surroundings with peeling paint, but a rigidly stable ideology. Now this does not matter as the Story of Berlin (see p84) covers most of what is here with verve, technology and a sense of interior design. Crowds still come to relive the Cold War and West Berlin as "an island of freedom". Artefacts linked with the great escapes are displayed here; these include cars with false bottoms, hot air balloons, bogus military uniforms and passports from non-existent countries.

Outside the museum, one watchtower remains on the Eastern side and an American warning sign has been left "in the West". America has, however, deliberately crossed the border; where thorough East German border checks used to take place is now the Checkpoint Charlie Business Center, an American–German joint venture. The Café Adler (see p157) remains too. John le Carré worked out his plots at this café and on 9 November 1989 it provided the first taste of the West for East Berliners streaming across.

Jüdisches Museum (Jewish Museum)
Lindenstr. 9-14, www.jmberlin.de *Mon 1000-2200, Tue-Sun
1000-2000. €5. U-Bahn Hallesches Tor.* Map 3, E1, p248

The architect Daniel Libeskind was first invited to Berlin in summer 1989 to design the museum. His family had lost 85 members in the Holocaust and his parents met as exiles in Samarkand, Uzbekistan. The main aim of the collection is to show 2,000 years of German-Jewish history, as well as the 12 years of Nazi persecution. It is a

Berlin border
The former Checkpoint Charlie, Berlin's most famous border crossing.

history that continued from 1945, and prior to 1933 was able to integrate into all aspects of German society. The layout is based on a broken, but not destroyed, Star of David. Those able to escape during the 1930s took, as well as the personal mementoes show here, knowledge and attachment to an earlier Germany which would in due course return. In most cases the few photos and letters shown here would be their only link with their former families.

The building without the exhibits opened in 1999 and attracted half a million visitors in a year. One area, a closed dark triangle has been left as a void to symbolize the destruction caused by the

★ **Best**

Romantic spots

Holocaust. Others are deliberately crowded to show what could be packed into an émigré's suitcase and equally, the vibrancy of 19th-century Jewish society, and that which is now being re-established.

★ Topographie des Terrors (Outline of Terror)

Niederkirchnerstr., www.topographie.de *Daily 1000-1800. Free. S-Bahn Anhalter Bahnhof. Map 6, D7, p253*

It would never be easy to decide what to do with the remains of the buildings along the former Prinz-Albrecht-Strasse where Nazi extermination policies were planned and implemented. Heinrich Himmler, the head of the SS, had his offices here and the buildings were also used to imprison, torture and execute opponents of the regime.

The buildings were largely in what would become East Berlin, but as Niederkirchnerstrasse, the new name of the street, became the border, that area was cleared in 1961 to make way for the Wall and its backup. There was little interest in the West in studying the Nazi period at that time so although it was known that cells from the prison stretched into what became West Berlin, they were not excavated until the 1980s.

The temporary exhibition set up then has now become rather permanent. It is all in the open air with placards outside the cells explaining the history of the SS. The planned building for covering this site is one of the many casualties of Berlin's ongoing financial crisis. There is a forlorn hope that it might be open on 8 May 2005, the 60th anniversary of the end of the Second World War.

This is also the best place to view the former Wall, as a long stretch has been preserved here, and was protected as a cultural monument before too many souvenir hunters had chipped away mementoes. A few other remnants remain, but the overall planning policy has been to eliminate as far as possible all evidence of this former division. The only concession to history is a line of bricks built into the roads in this area that follows the exact line of the former Wall. It can be seen in front of the Brandenburg Gate, across the Potsdamer Platz and on Friedrichstrasse at the former Checkpoint Charlie.

Neue Gesellschaft Für Bildende Kunst (NGBK) (New Society for Visual Art)

Oranienstr. 25, **T** 615 30 31, www.ngbk.de *Daily 1200-1830. U-Bahn Kottbusser Tor. Map 3, E4, p248*

Situated on the colourful Oranienstrasse, NGBK has exhibited a great range of contemporary art, from the photographers Wolfgang Tillmans and Hannah Villiger, to exhibitions exploring identity and security in the modern age.

East Side Gallery

Running along Mühlenstr. to Warschauerstr., www.eastsidegallery.com *U-Bahn Warschauer Str., U-Bahn Schlesisches Tor. Map 3, D8, p249*

Possibly the most historical gallery site in the whole of Germany. It is one of the last remaining areas where the Wall still stands and is situated to the east of Kreuzberg on the border with Friedrichshain. The Wall was given to artists around the world

Fallen Leaves

Thousands of small iron faces – Shalechet (Fallen Leaves) – form an installation by Menashe Kadsihman. Placed in an eerie 'void', one of the tall angular spaces which cut right through the Jewish museum, they are spread out on the floor and disappear into a black hole at the far end of the space.

to paint a series of murals, varying from the hope of peace to the famous Trabant car, and Erich Honecker (the leader of the East German Communist Party) kissing Leonid Brezhnev (the general secretary of the USSR).

Museum der verbotenen Kunst – Grenzwachtum (Museum of Forbidden Art – Border Watchtower)

Puschkinallee Guard Post, **T** 532 00 09. *Daily 1200-1800. Free. U-Bahn Schlesisches Tor. Map 3, G10, p249*

The Puschkinallee Guard Post is the nearest experience to reliving East Germany that a modern visitor can get. Clamber up the tower and look west at what was for 28 years the forbidden fruit. Picture yourself standing there for eight hours a day, or perhaps a night, with two other equally bored colleagues, trying to concentrate on the emptiness below. National service normally required a year of this border duty, which involved total inactivity in most cases, but which was occasionally interspersed with the need to shoot at those attempting to escape. All the furnishings in the tower have been left intact, and on the lower floors, changing exhibitions are shown of artists whose work could not pass the censor in East German times.

Deutsches Technikmuseum (German Science Museum)

Trebbinerstr. 9, www.dtmb.de *Tue-Fri 0900-1730, Sat-Sun 1000-1800. €3. U-Bahn Möckernbrücke. Map 4, G10, p251*

This is appropriately housed in the former goods-yard of Anhalter Station, one of Berlin's largest before the war. Transport still forms the basis of the collection, going back to the pre-science of the stagecoach and forward to space travel. Public and luxury private travel sit side by side and both sides of the war are represented with the aircraft on show. The Spectrum Centre is the draw for all children; the sounds and the ever-changing colours bring many aspects of science to life, and touching all the exhibits is actively encouraged. A new aviation gallery will open in summer 2003.

Schwules Museum (Museum of Homosexuality)
Mehringdamm 61, **T** 69 31 172, www.schwulesmuseum.de
Wed-Mon 1400-1800. €4. U-Bahn Mehringdamm.   Map 4, H12, p251

It is appropriate that Berlin, where homosexuals suffered as much as Jews under the Nazi regime, has a proper environment to show gay history as well as the current gay scene. For younger people the museum will be a salutary reminder of how recently homosexuality was banned and ridiculed. It is perhaps significant that the museum has never received official funding and only in 2002 was it able to allocate some space for a permanent collection. It is still, however, better known for its temporary exhibitions of art by the gay community. Some of these are linked with their lifestyles, and some not.

Zehlendorf

Money does not just grow on trees here, it flows in all directions. Londoners will appreciate why it is twinned with Hampstead. Everything is on a grand scale with even the railway stations being individually designed. It grew up as a transit stop between royal Berlin and royal Potsdam, being exactly 14 kilometres from each. Slightly more ordinary people are seen now, but they are smart seven days a week. Expect designer shops rather than supermarkets, villa colonies rather than blocks of flats, wine rather than beer.

Luckily even the rich use buses and trains, so walking here is always a pleasure, never a necessity. At the station now called Mexicoplatz, the restored Jugendstil interior is ample compensation for missing a train. Cycling is even nicer, with paths around the lakes, and too few cars to cause pollution. Factories are of course totally banished. Several villas are now museums, and no famous architect from the

1920s failed to leave his mark in Zehlendorf. One museum is in fact totally in the open air. Other visits include the eccentric palaces of minor royalty and senior Nazis.

◉ Sights

★ Alliierten Museum (The Allies Museum)
Clayallee 135, www.alliiertenmuseum.de Thu-Tue 1000-1800. Free. U-Bahn Oskar-Helene-Heim. Map 8, p256

It is now hard to realize that the theme of this museum only became history in 1994 when the American, British and French "occupation" troops left Berlin. Inevitably the museum is a Cold War period piece, but as there is only one other in Berlin (the Checkpoint Charlie museum) it is none the worse for that. The films it shows are as important as its exhibits and it covers the whole period from 1945 when this occupation started.

The museum was opened in 1998 to commemorate the 50th anniversary of the blockade between June 1948 and May 1949 when the Russians closed the road, rail and canal links to West Germany. The allies organized a continuous airlift to supply West Berlin with goods with planes usually taking off and landing every minute, day and night. The museum is large enough to house aircraft, tanks, searchlights and the guardhouse formerly situated at Checkpoint Charlie.

Brücke Museum
Bussardteig 9, www.brueckemuseum.de Wed-Mon 1100-1900. €4. U-Bahn Oskar-Helene-Heim. Map 8, p256

Tragedy gave this quiet and isolated museum international prominence in April 2002 when thieves stole nine paintings in a 10-minute raid. Die Brücke (The Bridge) is the name of an artistic school, initially close to Expressionism, which was founded in Dresden in 1905 and then based in Berlin until the outbreak of the First World War.

Perhaps better known for what they despised than what they stood for, it was subsequent Nazi hatred and persecution that ensured for them a worldwide and long-lasting reputation. Initially they concentrated on rural landscapes and on nudes; then several of them turned to urban backgrounds and pioneered the use of woodcuts. On the few occasions when works of artists such as Erich Heckel and Ernst Ludwig Kirchner are offered for sale, they fetch millions. The location of the museum is deliberate, since it was where Arno Breker, the notorious Nazi sculptor and close partner of Albert Speer, had his studio.

Museumsdorf Düppel (Düppel Village Museum)
Clauerstr. 11, www.dueppel.de *Sun Apr-Oct 1000-1700. Check the website for details of midweek openings. €2. S-Bahn Zehlendorf.* *Map 8, p256*

Visitors to eastern Europe will immediately feel at home in what they will know as an ethnographic museum. This one is, however, not an assembly of buildings from far and wide but an attempt to re-create exactly what was on this site. A bomb crater in 1940 revealed a village that clearly existed in the 12th century but seems to have been later abandoned. It was only in 1968 that excavation work started, in those days, in the shadow of the Berlin Wall. Several houses have now been rebuilt and the great commitment in Germany to environmental issues has ensured support for the weaving, baking and even sheep-rearing that now takes place here. The articles sold here are original and politically correct souvenirs.

Pfaueninsel (Peacock Island)

The castle is open Tue-Sun 1000-1700. €3. S-Bahn Wannsee then bus 216 or 316. Boats cross to the island every 30 mins from 0800 till 2000. €1. Map 8, p256

Friedrich Wilhelm III was on the throne for 43 years from 1797 till 1840 with many military and architectural achievements to his name, but Berliners will always remember him as the monarch who opened a palace to the public and in this case a whole island as well. Much would be novel to them, in particular the fountains and the palm trees and the peacocks which give the island its name. Less tastefully, a negro, a giant and two dwarfs were also brought in as servants and as curiosities for the visitors. It was a royal escape from the formal courts in Berlin and Potsdam so the house is less elaborate and the gardens more casual, even though they were designed by Peter Joseph Lenné (1789-1866), famous for his landscaping at most of the Berlin and Potsdam palaces. Little restoration has been necessary as there was no damage in the Second World War.

The house is probably unique as a royal residence in having only eight rooms and being built entirely of wood. However casual life was here, certain proprieties had to be maintained. The servants' quarters, although also designed by Schinkel, are apart from the main building, as is the kitchen to protect the house from the danger of fire. An underground passage leads from the kitchen into the main house, which prevented a servant and his master casually bumping into each other in the gardens. Although senior Nazis entertained here frequently, they fortunately made no alterations to any of the buildings.

Museums and Galleries

- **Ägyptisches Museum** Egyptian collection, p88.
- **Alliierten Museum** What the American and British forces got up to during their post-war occupation of West Berlin, p104.
- **Altes Museum** The luxury and style of ancient Greece, reflected in its jewellery, p56.
- **Alte Nationalgalerie** 19th-century German art, all finally under one roof, p57.
- **Bauhaus-Archiv** Drawings of what Germany's most famous architects achieved and hoped to achieve, p71.
- **Bröhan Museum** If it was stylish in Berlin houses before the war it is here, p90.
- **Brücke Museum** Paintings of the group Hitler hated most, housed in the villa of his favourite sculptor, p104.
- **Deutsche Historische Museum** Reopening in early 2004, German history warts and all, p49.
- **Deutsches Technikmuseum** Stage coach transport to space travel, p102.
- **East Side Gallery** Painted remainder of Berlin Wall, p100.
- **Eigen + Art** Gallery promoting East German artists, p79.
- **Erotik Museum** Some innocent exhibits and some definitely not, p70.
- **Friedrichswerdersche Kirche (Schinkel Museum)** Schinkel's drawings housed in converted church, p46.
- **Forschungs- und Gedenkstätte Normannenstrasse (Stasi Museum)** The secret police uncovered, p62.
- **Galerie Bodo Niemann** Sleek, modern photography gallery, p79.
- **Gemäldegalerie** The best of German painting from the 13th to the 18th century, p92.
- **Hamburger Bahnhof** Current German art which nobody else will handle, p67.

● Museums and Galleries

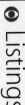
Listings

- **Haus am Checkpoint Charlie** What happened below, through and above the Berlin Wall, p97.
- **Jüdisches Museum** 2,000 years of Jewish history in Germany, p97.
- **Käthe-Kollwitz Museum** Genteel surroundings for Berlin's most famous political artist, p82.
- **Knoblauchhaus** Overflowing with 19th-century affluence and taste, p59.
- **Kunstgewerbemuseum** Applied arts from stained glass to laptop computers, p93.
- **Kunstwerke BERLIN (Institute for Contemporary Art)**, Factory-turned-art house for installations, p77.
- **Museumdorf Düppel** A medieval village brought back to life, p105.
- **Museum für Kommunikation** Everything from post-horses to email, p48.
- **Neue Gesellschaft Für Bildende Kunst (NGBK) (New Society for Visual Art)** Venue for variety of contemporary art, p100.
- **Neue Nationalgalerie** 20th-century German painting in appropriately modern surroundings, p93.
- **Pergamon Museum** The best of Turkey and the best of Babylon, p56.
- **Sammlung Berggruen** The Picasso museum which saves a visit both to Paris and to the French Riviera, p89.
- **Schwules Museum** Homosexual museum, p103.
- **Story of Berlin** Exactly that, with all the fun and the horror in equal measure, p84.
- **Topographie des Terrors** The grim detail of SS Headquarters in Berlin, p99.
- **Vitra Design Museum** What trend-setters have in their homes and offices, p77.

Potsdam 111 The royal family escaped revolutions here, Berliners now escape stress and noise for garden walks, classical concerts and exuberant architecture.

Köpenick 119 A double retreat, into history and into the countryside. Its palace has the best in German design over the last 10 centuries, its rivers and lakes provide an escape from the hectic capital.

Potsdam

Potsdam has always provided an escape from Berlin. In the 18th century, Frederick the Great, trying to be more French than the French, hoped to run a court there similar to the one Louis XIV had established a century earlier in Versailles. For Friedrich Wilhelm IV in the 19th century, however, it was different. He knew that however turbulent the mob would become in Berlin, the Potsdam garrison would protect him and his lifestyle. For the victors at the end of the Second World War, planning the future of Germany in July 1945, the **Cecilienhof Palace** provided a luxurious refuge from all the surrounding devastation. For East Germans, it was like the Baltic republics to the Russians, a "near abroad" providing glimpses of a world they would never otherwise see. Now the escapes are daily; commuters unwilling to restrict themselves to a flat near their office buy the houses which Soviet officers had to give up on German reunification.

Although written documentation on Potsdam goes back about 1,000 years, it was Frederick the Great who converted a small textile centre into a unique display of ostentation and military power by building a **palace** and a **barracks** here. Both would continue to play equal roles in the town's history until 1990. Not until then did the military retreat, certain that Potsdam could assert its past without their presence.

▸▸ See Sleeping p137

The main station in Potsdam (Potsdam Hauptbahnhof) is reached by the S-Bahn 7 from Zoo Station (30 mins) and a network of local railways, buses and trams connect the various sights. A more original way to arrive is to take a bus to Schloss Glienicke, walk across the Glienicke Bridge (previously only opened for swapping spies) and then to take a local tram. For tours, tickets and information see p31.

Welcome to the pleasure palace

Sans Souci displays electic architectural styles reflecting the varied tastesof Frederick the Great

◉ Sights

Sans Souci
Tue-Sun 0900-1700. €8. S-Bahn Potsdam Hauptbahnhof,
then bus 695. Map 8, p256

The French name, meaning carefree, which Frederick the Great
chose for his palace, sums up much of what took place there.
Whether the rooms are of marble or wood, decorated in a Roman
or Greek style, it is clear that this is a palace of pleasure, not of
work. It also shows how international a figure Frederick the Great
was. If he conquered his neighbours militarily, he drew from them
culturally, and this palace is a reflection of his varied tastes. The
back entrance, which is used for visitors, gives no idea of its
opulence. It is better viewed from the terraces at the front, which
is how visitors would have originally first seen it. The library is the
only modest room of the 12 shown and, significantly, many more
books are in French than in German. The designs in the Voltaire
room result from the bitter end of his three-year stay in Potsdam.
They show monkeys and parrots, with whom Frederick the Great
equated him.

   Frederick the Great is now buried just outside the palace as he
had wished. He had first been buried in the city, then was taken
to western Germany at the end of the Second World War, before
being brought back here in 1991 to join his dogs, whose tombs
had never been moved.

Neues Palais (New Palace)
Sat-Thu 0900-1700. €6. S-Bahn Park Sanssouci then bus 695.
Map 8, p256

This was Frederick's reward to himself for his successful military
campaigns during the Seven Years' War (1756-63). It has 200

The riddle of Sans Souci

On the outside ledge of the dome at Sans Souci, its name can clearly be read "SANS, SOUCI". Why though the comma? Its insertion was deliberate since it can be seen as clearly as any of the letters.

One interpretation is that guests stayed in the rooms to the left of the comma whereas Frederick the Great stayed in those on the right. He therefore had the *souci*, the worries or concerns, whereas his guests did not. Another theory links the comma to secret religious codes of the 18th century, when it represented calvinism as opposed to deism which is represented by a full stop. Therefore no calvinism meant no worries.

Inevitably, one theory has to bring in sex, as no work on Frederick is complete without extensive speculation in this field. He was sterile, so produced no heirs. Given what a comma might be taken to represent, it is no wonder that the riddle remains unsolved 250 years later.

rooms and a theatre. Sandstone is the predominant material for many of the statues, which shows the meagre finances available at the end of this war. One room, however, was decorated in marble from Carrara in Italy. The most unusual room is decorated as a grotto. This started fairly modestly with a collection of shells and corals but by the end of the 19th century was embellished with minerals and jewels. The members of the royal family who lived in Britain introduced baths and flushing toilets to the building during the 19th century. The theatre, modelled on a Roman amphitheatre, holds around 300 people and is used frequently for concerts during the summer months. The Communs, the building behind the Palace, were servants' quarters.

Chinesisches Haus (Chinese Tea House)

Tue-Sun 1000-1700. €1. S-Bahn Potsdam Hauptbahnhof then bus 695. Map 8, p256

This is the caricature that was to appear all over Western Europe during the 18th century. China is portrayed as a land of constant tea- drinking and music-making, interspersed with an occasional walk under a parasol. The porcelain exhibited is also from this period.

Orangerie

Tue-Sun 1000-1700. €1. S-Bahn Potsdam Hauptbahnhof then bus 695. Map 8, p256

Dating from the 1850s, the Orangerie design shows the emperor Friedrich Wilhelm IV was as infatuated with Italy as Frederick the Great had been with France. The architect August Stüler, Schinkel's most famous pupil, was clearly influenced by the design of the Uffizi in Florence. It is worth climbing the tower since this gives the best view of the whole park. The façade is 300 m long, about the same length as the New Palace, so presumably Friedrich Wilhelm felt the need to endow Potsdam with a building as grand as that left by Frederick the Great. It was used to entertain and to accommodate guests of the Kaiser, including the Russian royal family.

Schloss Cecilienhof (Cecilienhof Palace)

0900-1700. €5. S-Bahn Potsdam Hauptbahnhof then bus 692. Map 8, p256

Built during the First World War for the son and daughter-in-law of the Kaiser, it took the latter's name, Cecilie. Although they went into exile with the rest of the family in 1918, they were allowed to return in 1923 and stayed until April 1945. It is clearly modelled both outside and inside on a "stockbroker Tudor" English country house. In the simplicity of its design and the modesty of its furnishings, it could not be a greater contrast to the other Potsdam palaces. Princess Cecilie was keen on yachting, which explains the decor of several rooms.

The palace is best known as the setting for the Potsdam Conference in July 1945 when the three allied powers confirmed the post-war fate of Germany. Many rooms have been left exactly as they were then and the table at which the treaty was signed is among many contemporary exhibits. By around 2000 the gardens had been restored to their original condition. As the former border to West Berlin ran along the shore of the lake, the defence installations which the East Germans set up, led to the removal of most of the trees. The new administration of Potsdam is proud of the 10,000 trees planted since 1990, many at the former border. The palace is now a luxury hotel; its restaurant regularly serves the "neutral" menu prepared for the conference – Russian fish soup, American steak and British whisky syllabub.

Holländisches Viertel (Dutch Quarter)
S-Bahn Potsdam Hauptbahnhof. Map 8, p256

The last major RAF raid over Germany struck Potsdam on 14 April 1945; as with the attack on Dresden two months earlier, it savagely damaged the town but did not destroy it. In the case of Potsdam, only the town and not the palaces was hit. Much restoration was done towards the end of the East German regime during the 1980s. The pace of this increased after reunification, greatly encouraged by developers who quickly saw the commercial potential. The Dutch Quarter now shows the results. Restoration has been so effective that this area is second only to Prague in its use as a film set.

! The last kaiser, Kaiser Wilhelm II, is thought to have hated Berlin so much that he said comparing it to Paris or London was like comparing beer to champagne.

Friedrich Wilhelm I went to Holland in 1732 to recruit masons and woodworkers and civil engineers. The royal family had already married into their Dutch opposite numbers so this was not a particularly surprising move. The canals, lakes and rivers in Potsdam gave rise to problems with which the Dutch were all too familiar. This quarter, which only has 150 houses in it, was built as an inducement for these recruits and was completed by 1749. Jan Bouman was the most famous recruit and his house at 8 Mittelstrasse is now a museum on the history of this area. The colourful stories told about Frederick the Great have led to a booming souvenir industry which displays its wares in this area. More serious visitors dismiss this material as "Fritz Kitsch".

Alexandrowka
S-Bahn Potsdam Hauptbahnhof then tram 90, 92 and 95. Map 8, p256

This small Russian settlement of 12 wooden houses dates from 1826 and is named after Czar Alexander I who had died in the previous year. In 1812 the Prussians, as reluctant allies of Napoleon, had taken prisoner about 60 Russians who were brought to Potsdam. Friedrich Wilhelm III liked Russian songs and a choir was formed for his benefit from this group. For the 12 still alive in 1826 these houses were built, following exact Russian models. Even their names were written in Cyrillic. The Alexander Nevsky Church, an equally faithful reproduction, was completed three years later in 1829.

Babelsberg Filmpark
August-Bebelstr., **T** 0331-7212755, **F** 0331-7212755, www.filmpark.de *Daily from 15 Mar-31 Oct 1000-1800. €15. S-Bahn Griebnitzsee (not Babelsberg which is a stop further on towards Potsdam). Map 8, p256*

The Babelsberg Filmpark has adapted better than any other Berlin institution to each change in regime. It was as important to the

East Germans as it had been to the Nazis and a quick privatization in the early 1990s made it an early and lasting beneficiary of reunification. For all too long, its productions were analysed for political trends, and mementoes of these earlier periods are displayed, but it is now an exciting day out for families and for the older still pretending to be young. The "Vulcano" crater is the high point of any visit where light and sound create an environment that nobody would want to experience in real life. Young children can be taken to the Sandmann-Studio to be greeted by elves and fairies whilst older ones can descend in a submarine. For adults, stick to the stunt shows and special effects. (Roman Polanski's 2002 award-winning *The Pianist* was part filmed at Babelsberg.)

Köpenick

Köpenick was a very necessary adjunct to East Berlin when the city was divided. It was all that the capital was not; it had ample gardens and lakes and still offered a small-town Germany that bombers and planners had destroyed in the town centre. The **Royal Palace** *here was not an embarrassment but a welcome embellishment. Foreigners are still rare here, but doubtless numbers will increase when the Old Town is completely restored, which should be during 2004.*

▸▸ *See Sleeping p138*

The S-Bahn station Köpenick is on the S3 line which starts at Ostbahnhof and the journey takes about 20 mins. However it is then necessary to take a bus or tram to the Old Town which is a good mile from the station. S-Bahn station Spindlersfeld is nearer, about half a mile from the Old Town and on a branch line from S-Bahn station Schöneweide which is served by several lines going into the town centre. In the summer, boats ply the Spree from Köpenick to the harbour at Treptow, close to the S-Bahn station of the same name.

◉ Sights

Town centre

S-Bahn Spindlersfeld. There is also an S-Bahn station called Köpenick, but it is further from the Castle and Old Town.   Map 8, p256

The **Schloss** (Palace) is due to reopen in summer 2003 together with its Applied Arts Museum. Unjustifiably Köpenick has never received the interest and commitment that Potsdam has done, even though its Old Town has survived and all major styles of architecture can be enjoyed there. Köpenick is particularly proud of the fact that it is older than Berlin, tracing its foundation to 1209. It is also quite happy to enjoy the fame given to it by the play *Captain of Köpenick*. This is based on the 1906 escapade of a recently released prisoner who managed to loot the town hall treasury simply by dressing up in military uniform and demanding access to the funds.

The palace in fact had a longer life as a teacher training college during the 19th century than as a royal residence in the 18th century, but amazingly its acres of baroque in the interior survived many different tenants and uses. In 1950, when the Royal Palace in Mitte was torn down, the furnishings were fortunately saved and they now form the basis of this collection. The high point is the silverware, which formed the royal dining service. Much of the collection, however, pre-dates the palace, including some 11th-century jewellery and 14th-century panelling. Since reunification, some items have been housed at the Kulturforum (see p90).

Yet quite apart from the palace, Köpenick appeals to modern visitors as a German town which the 20th century has not ravaged. Its other sites, such as the neo-gothic Rathaus Town Hall were commonplace in the 1930s but are now sadly rare. Narrow streets and fishermen's cottages are equally unexpected so close to Berlin.

In 1996 a statue to the "Captain" was unveiled in front of the Town Hall. Previous political regimes would not have dared to commemorate this affront to authority.

Berlin has a good selection of accommodation at either end of the spectrum but less choice in the middle. Its smarter hotels are often large and modern and some are at the cutting edge of contemporary design. There are also many traditional pensions, particularly on and around the Kurfürstendamm in Tiergarten and Charlottenburg in the centre of old West Berlin. Mitte, the hipper centre of united Berlin, has some good 'art hotels', where the building acts as exhibition space as well as hotel. The best of these are like staying in a gallery, though others attempt to latch on to the trend while being little more than hotels with a few pictures on the wall. Prenzlauerberg, now generally seen as being more of a creative hub than Mitte, has various excellent options and is not far from the centre. Friedrichshain has fewer hotels but is another alternative eastern possibility, with plenty of pre-unification atmosphere. Kreuzberg, once a lively area of West Berlin, is much quieter now, but retains interesting aspects and some decent places to stay with easy access to all the sights.

€ **Sleeping codes**

Price

LL	€300 and over	C	€100-149
L	€250-299	D	€75-99
A	€200-249	E	€51-74
B	€150-199	F	€50 and under

Prices are for a double room in high season

Hostels in Berlin are excellent: mostly modern, well-designed and well-equipped, they are a growing part of the market. In the best ones, a double room or apartment can be every bit as comfortable as in a hotel. Bed and breakfast in private homes is also becoming increasingly prevalent.

Seasons in the city are at best complex, at worst unfathomable. Berlin hotel prices have been compared to the stock market and the basic ranges given here are likely to be inflated for large trade fairs, conferences, the Film Festival and the Love Parade. Equally, most places are open to bartering down, especially if trade is quiet, and especially if you want to stay for a few days. If you're lucky or clever enough to visit the city with the right combination of factors, there are bargains to be had, even in the smartest hotels. It is also worth checking the websites for deals. Generally speaking, weekends are usually considered off-peak, and spring and autumn peak times. As in most German hotels, breakfast is often a big feature, and those with buffet breakfasts may lay on a feast of fruits, cereals, fresh bread, cheeses, cold meats and juices. Unless stated otherwise, breakfast is included. In most places, and certainly larger hotels and all hostels, staff speak English. In Potsdam and Köpenick this is less likely. When trying to find a hotel, bear in mind that street numbers generally go up one side and then down the other. Berlin's excellent public transport system means nowhere is too far from the centre and even places such as Köpenick or Potsdam are possibilities, neither more than 45 minutes from the centre.

Berlin Tourismus Marketing will book hotels for you for a €3 charge. It produces a brochure with most Berlin hotels, or you can book by phone, **T** 25 00 25, or through www.berlintourism.de For its three locations see Tourist Information, p33.

Mitte

Hotels and pensions

LL Adlon, Unter den Linden 77, **T** 22 61 0, **F** 22 61 22 22, www.hotel-adlon.de *S-Bahn Unter den Linden. Map 7, F2, p254* Right beside the Brandenburg Gate, the Adlon is far from discreet, but the stream of tourists peering past the behatted doormen doesn't seem to deter a regular turnover of celebrities. They follow in hallowed footsteps: Albert Einstein, Charlie Chaplin and Theodore Roosevelt all stayed here at a time when it was one of Europe's most prominent luxury addresses. The current building, built after the fall of the wall, is, however, a replica of the original, damaged by fire in the Second World War. The opulence is as showy as you might expect, but also impressively stylish. The light, open, cream-coloured lobby has a stained glass cupola and fountains. Rooms, some of which look straight out at the Brandenburg Gate, have cherrywood trim, black marble bathrooms and data ports.

LL Four Seasons Hotel, Charlottenstr. 49, **T** 20 33 8, **F** 20 33 61 66, www.fourseasons.com *U-Bahn Französische Str. Map 7, F5, p254.* Externally unremarkable, but inside the Four Seasons, however, it's all marble, Viennese crystal chandeliers, soft furnishings and soft music. Service is attentive and the sumptuousness and cosy elegance extends into the bedrooms: enormous marble bathrooms, big, comfortable beds, thick towels, expensive toiletries and excellent views of the Französischer Dom all remind you just how much luxury you're getting.

A-B art'otel, Wallstr. 70-73, **T** 24 06 20, **F** 24 06 22 22, www.artotels.de *U-Bahn Märkisches Museum. Map 7, H11, p255* This largely business-orientated hotel is filled with the work of German contemporary artist Georg Baselitz, giving it a memorable edge, and attracting a creative clientele that the hotel might otherwise leave cold. Three massive monoprints welcome you when you walk in and the hotel has some 540 other works, though not all are originals. Austrian architect Johanne Nalbach has cleverly covered the space between the new building and the rococo Ermerlerhaus and made it into a covered courtyard restaurant.

B-C Artist Hotel Riverside, Friedrichstr. 106, **T** 28 49 00, **F** 28 49 049, www.tolles-hotel.de *U-Bahn and S-Bahn Friedrichstr. Map 2, H4, p246* Given the 'designed by artists for artists' premise of this hotel, you might expect something a little more left field. Instead, what you get is a fairly conventional hotel, albeit one in a prime position on the river. Rooms not facing the river can be a bit gloomy and antique telephones in rooms don't do enough to compensate for the overuse of peach paint. The cheaper and more arty **Artist Pension-Hotel Die Loge**, up the road near Oranienburger Tor station at number 115 is run by the same people. It is due to re-open in summer 2003.

B-C Hackescher Markt, Grosse Präsidentenstr. 8, **T** 28 00 30, **F** 28 00 31 11, www.hackescher-markt.com *S-Bahn Hackescher Markt. Map 7, C8, p255* In a great position, on a relatively quiet road right in the midst of Berlin's liveliest area, staying here is money well spent. Staff are professional, enthusiastic and helpful and the rooms are luxurious. Beds, even the single ones, are large, the shiny bathrooms have heated floors, there's a pretty courtyard and rooms at the top of the building have good views over Berlin. There's even a bar at street level, as well, of course, as plenty of others nearby.

B-D Künstlerheim Luise, Luisenstr. 19, **T** 28 44 80, **F** 28 06 942, www.kuenstlerheim-luise.de *U-Bahn Friedrichstr. Map 7, C2, p254* Plain on the outside but self-consciously groovy on the inside, Künstlerheim Luise's rooms are all individually designed and decorated by different artists. Those on the top floor are basic and small, though still colourful. Rooms further down are grander. The concept works better in some rooms than in others: some feel like being inside works of modern art, some more like being in an IKEA catalogue. One possible downside is the proximity of the train line: S-Bahns trundle past the first floor.

C Honigmond Garden Hotel, Invalidenstr. 122, **T** 28 44 55 77, **F** 28 44 55 88, www.honigmond-berlin.de *S-Bahn Nordbahnhof. Map 2, F4, p246* The Honigmond Garden Hotel (sibling of the Honigmond Restaurant-Hotel, below) is a cosy place. It is in an attractive building, built in 1845, and facing one of east Berlin's bigger barren spaces. Stripped wooden doors and floors, iron framed beds and a suit of armour contrast with a sunny and verdant garden courtyard. The hotel recently won a Berlin 'Gastro-Award' for its food.

C-E Honigmond Restaurant-Hotel, Borsigstr. 28, **T** 28 44 550, **F** 28 44 55 11, www.honigmond-berlin.de *S-Bahn Nordbahnhof. Map 2, F4, p246* On a quiet street, the Honigmond Restaurant-Hotel is more of a pension than a hotel: rooms, albeit light, airy and homely ones, above an excellent restaurant and café, with good cakes. The whole place has a pleasantly young, laid-back feel. Breakfast is not included in the good value prices.

D Hotel Taunus, Monbijouplatz 1, **T** 28 35 254, **F** 28 35 255, www.hotel-taunus.de *S-Bahn Hackescher Markt. Map 7, C8, p255* Taunus has made a feature out of its external fire-escape stairs, which wind down the outside of a striking pale building. The clean modern design is continued inside in the simple en suite rooms.

D-E mitArt Pension, Friedrichstr. 127, **T** 28 39 04 30, **F** 28 39 04 32. *U-Bahn Oranienburger Tor. Map 7, B4, p254* An exceptionally friendly and memorably stylish hotel. Still primarily a gallery, the owner originally rented out rooms to exhibiting artists and has now expanded the concept so that hotel guests sit having breakfast among works of modern art suspended from the ceiling. Service is personal, breakfast is copious and delicious and rooms are homely and well decorated.

E Hotel am Scheunenviertel, Oranienburger Str. 38, **T** 28 22 12 52 830, **F** 28 21 115. *U-Bahn Oranienburger Tor. Map 7, B5, p254* This good value Jewish quarter hotel has plain, modern rooms and a rather plain breakfast, but it's well-placed near Friedrichstrasse and within walking distance of Unter den Linden. Although it's not over endowed with character, service is helpful and friendly. It's also surprisingly quiet at night, considering the nightclub next door.

Hostels

E-F Circus Hostels, Rosa-Luxemburg-Str. 39-41 and Weinbergs-weg 1a, **T** 28 39 14 33, **F** 28 39 14 84, www.circus-berlin.de *U-Bahn Rosa-Luxemburg-Platz and U-Bahn Rosenthaler Platz respectively. Map 7, B11, p255 and Map 2, F6, p246* A second Circus Hostel has now opened in the city, a good pointer to the fact that this blueprint is everything a good hostel should be. Wooden floors and metal-framed beds complement a simple, bright and modern decor. Staff are friendly, helpful, English-speaking or even English and print the day's news and weather from the internet and put them up on a noticeboard. Both locations have bars with DJs and late opening and breakfast is a generous buffet for only €3.50. The atmosphere is young and enthusiastic without being too in-your-face. And the loft apartments in the Weinbergsweg hostel, complete with roof terraces and kitchens, rival almost anywhere in the city for views and comfort.

Tiergarten

Hotels

L-B Grand Hyatt, Marlene-Dietrich-Platz, **T** 25 53 12 34, **F** 25 53 12 35, www.berlin.hyatt.com *S-Bahn and U-Bahn Potsdamer Platz, U-Bahn Mendelssohn-Bartholdy-Park. Map 6, C4, p253* This is a superb combination of Oriental and Bauhaus deluxe minimalism. The angular lines of Potsdamer Platz itself are continued into the interior: the lobby is a stunning space, with a flower bed of seasonal blooms offsetting the harsh acute angles. The Feng Shui of the corridor carpet design (frantic along the corridors, but calm at the ends, apparently) might not do much for you, but more useful and personal design minutiae are everywhere. Special drains mean you can deliberately overflow your bath and fresh fruit and novels in English are provided in each room. You can use the TV for Play-station games or to pay your bill and there's a button inside the door to light up a 'do not disturb' sign outside. On Sundays you don't have to check out until 1800. A roof-top health club and pool have great views and the service is exceptional. Prices sky-rocket during the Berlin Film Festival. If you can manage to get a room at that time, you will probably be able to look out of the window at Hollywood's finest as they troop into the cinema opposite.

Prenzlauerberg

Hotels and pensions

B-C Myer's, Metzer Str. 26, **T** 44 01 40, **F** 44 01 41 04, www.myershotel.de *U-Bahn Senefelderplatz. Map 2, F8, p247* Diethard Meusel's photos, displayed throughout the hotel, lift this place from its otherwise rather ordinary modern decor. Unfortunately some of the paintings that decorate the remainder are as awful as Meusel's pictures are good. Art aside, this isn't a bad place at all though. The lobby has antique furniture and a bar that's open 24/7. All rooms look inwards to a garden and courtyard and are therefore quiet, and breakfast in summer can be had outside. Rooms on the top (fifth) floor have baths and views.

C-D Hotel Jurine, Schwedter Str. 15, **T** 44 32 990, **F** 44 32 99 99, www.hotel-jurine.de *U-Bahn Senefelderplatz. Map 2, E7, p247* In summer the well-placed Jurine has an excellent garden terrace. In winter you'll have to make do with the eight different types of breakfast cereal on offer. The 53 rooms are plush, modern and quiet and there's a double specially designed for the disabled. If you baulk at the €12 extra for the large buffet breakfast, there's an excellent Italian café-trattoria just a couple of doors down the road.

E Transit Loft, Greifswalderstr. 219 (entrance on Immanuel-kirchstrasse), **T** 48 49 37 73, **F** 44 05 10 74, www.transit-loft.de *U-Bahn Senefelderplatz. Map 2, F10, p247* A large, open, colourful space greets you out of the lift when you arrive at this modern hostel. Built in 2001, good use is made of both natural and artificial light and there are only a few enormous pipes along the corridor ceilings to remind visitors of its history as a factory. There's a generous buffet breakfast available until noon and a massive billiard room downstairs has 37 tables.

Hostels

F Mitte's Backpacker Hostel, Chaussestr. 102, **T** 28 39 09 65, **F** 28 39 09 35, www.backpacker.de *U-Bahn Zinnowitzer Str. Map 2, F3, p246* Dirty, smelly steps leading up from the street to this hostel might not give the best first impression, but once inside it's an oasis of colour and friendly welcome. The common area has large, comfy beanbags and a sunny eating area. There's a TV room, internet access, bike hire, table football and you can get good coffee as well as lots of advice (in excellent English) from reception. Rooms, in all sizes from single upwards, are individually designed and most have themes: all are cheerfully colourful. The 'Aquarium Room' has hanging papier maché fish and a mermaid, while the 'Honeymoon Suite' has padded hearts and hanging veils (but, bizarrely, two single beds). Your only complaint might be the lumpy pillows.

Apartments for rent

C-D acksel Haus, Belforter Str. 21, **T** 44 33 76 33, www.ackselhaus.de *U-Bahn Senefelderplatz. Map 2, F9, p247* Some of the 16 apartments on this quiet tree-lined street are among the most attractive living areas you will find. Remarkably good value, they are enormous, classy spaces with antique furniture, wooden floors and large, sunny windows. Most have separate living rooms and kitchens. Loosely themed, each apartment is different: the Movie apartment is decorated with black and white cinema photos and has a collection of antique projectors; Venice has Venetian wallpaper, while Rome has warm colours and drawings of the city. Breakfast is not included.

Friedrichshain

Hostels

F Pegasus Hostel, Str. der Pariser Kommune 35, **T** 29 35 18 10, **F** 29 35 11 66, www.pegasushostel.de *S-Bahn Ostbahnhof, U-Bahn Weberwiese. Map 3, B9, p249* In an atmospheric old east Berlin building which was once a Jewish girls' boarding school, this hostel is rough around the edges, but friendly, sociable and good value. There are plans for a sauna and entertainment room. Dorm beds start at €13.

Charlottenburg

Hotels and pensions

L-A Hotel Brandenburger Hof, Eislebenerstr. 14, **T** 21 40 50,
F 21 40 51 00, www.brandenburger-hof.com *U-Bahn Augsburger
Strasse U-Bahn Kurfürstendamm. Map 4, F3, p250* One of the city's
top luxury hotels is on a quiet, anonymous street south of Breitscheidplatz. The grand late 19th-century façade and lobby contrast
with the sleek and elegant modernism of the Bauhaus-influenced
rooms upstairs. Everything about the place is effortlessly stylish,
from the light and airy surrounds of the Wintergarten piano bar to
the rich, clubby atmosphere of the library. The restaurant, Die
Quadriga, has been awarded a Michelin star for its fine French
cuisine. The pampering reaches new heights in the Thaleia
massage and beauty suite while the friendly and attentive service
is epitomised by touches such as fresh apples in the lobby.

L-C Hotel Gates, Knessebeckstr. 8-9, **T** 31 10 06, **F** 31 22 060,
www.hotel-gates.com *U-Bahn Ernst-Reuter-Pl. Map 4, C1, p250*
Claiming to be the first hotel in Europe to have free 24-hour
internet access in every room, the recently overhauled Hotel
Gates is a cleverly marketed combination of old (the 1950s
breakfast room remains unaltered, though implausibly shiny)
and new. Service is friendly. Book online for lower prices.

A-B Bleibtreu Hotel, Bleibtreustr. 31, **T** 88 47 40, **F** 88 47 44 44,
www.bleibtreu.com *S-Bahn Savignyplatz. Map 4, E1, p250* The
Bleibtreu experience includes a florist, café and "wellness centre"
as part of its grand scheme. Though some of the gobbledygook
("dreaming fortifies the soul") used to justify the concept borders
on the self-righteous, it's hard to deny the effectiveness of the
design. Hyper-modern lighting and natural materials combine

with specially designed Italian furniture and enormous quantities of glass beads to very slick effect. You can even set the TV to wake you up in the morning. The breakfast buffet is €15 extra.

B-C Hotel Art Nouveau, Leibnizstr. 59, **T** 32 77 440, **F** 32 77 440, www.hotelartnouveau.de *U-Bahn Adenauerplatz. Map 4, E1, p250* This friendly and helpful fourth floor hotel is in a restored art nouveau era building with well designed contemporary touches and some original features. Beds and bathrooms (cleverly built into rooms to take advantage of natural light and not interfere with the original ceilings) are modern, furniture is antique and floors are wooden. The buffet breakfast is in a sunny room. There is also an 'honesty bar' which guests can tuck into at any time.

B-C Ku'Damm 101, Kurfürstendamm 101, **T** 52 00 550, **F** 52 00 55 555, www.kudamm101.com *U-Bahn Adenauerplatz. Map 4, E1, p250* This boldly modern hotel opened in January 2003. With ample business facilities, the prime target is clearly trade fair- and conference-goers. However the Ku'Damm would also make a good out-of-centre base. Whereas modern hotels in the city centre tend to use angles, the Ku'Damm's signature is the curve. With a modern minimalist take on vaguely 70s and 50s themes, seating, the bar and the (especially groovy) TVs are all curved and most furniture is adjustable and movable. Le Corbusier colours and coloured lighting add to the tight design. Even the buffet breakfast (in a seventh floor room with spectacular views of the city) is visually striking.

C Hotel Askanischer Hof, Kurfürstendamm 53, **T** 88 18 033, **F** 88 17 206, www.askanischer-hof.de *S-Bahn Savignyplatz. Map 4, E1, p250* This hotel predates the Second World War and tries to retain a 1930s feel. This is mainly successful: large, sunny rooms have antique furniture and very shiny bathrooms. Some touches, however, such as pictures on toilet seats, and third-rate art in the corridors, detract from the generally classy feel.

C-D Propeller Island City Lodge, Albrecht-Achilles-Str. 58, **T** 89 19 016, **F** 89 28 721, www.propeller-island.com *U-Bahn Adenauerplatz. Map 4, E1, p250* Almost certainly the most extraordinary hotel you will ever stay in, Propeller Island City Lodge is mind-boggling, amusing and visually stunning in equal part. Each of the 32 rooms is a painstakingly conceived and brilliantly realised piece of fantasy and sculpted work of art, from the Distorted Room, where the floor steeply slopes and nothing is quite right to the Dwarves Room, only 1.4 m high and full of small woodland people. Each room has a stereo which can play specially composed 'sonic sculptures'. Breakfast is an extra €7. To book, send a fax stating a choice of three rooms. Check the rooms on the website. Since reception is only open from 0800-1200, you should also give your time of arrival as precisely as possible.

C-E Hotel Charlot am Kurfürstendamm, Giesebrechtstr. 17, **T** 32 79 660, **F** 32 79 66 66, www.hotel-charlot.de *U-Bahn Adenauerplatz. Map 4, E1, p250* On a wide tree-lined street with golfing and sailing shops, this might feel a long way from the cutting edge of contemporary Berlin, but it's still only a short walk from the Ku'damm and not more than 20 minutes from Bahnhof Zoo. It's also a bright, friendly and attractive if blandly decorated place. Rooms without en suite facilities are especially good value.

C-E Pension Dittberner, Wielandstr. 26, **T** 88 46 950, **F** 88 54 046. *U-Bahn Adenauerplatz, S-Bahn Savignyplatz. Map 4, F1, p250* Recent winner of the 'most friendly pension in Berlin' prize, this is indeed a very welcoming place to stay, in a quiet street off Kurfürstendamm. The style is distinctly German, despite the oriental prints which combine with contemporary art on the walls. Some rooms are palatial, one with a grand balcony, and even the standard doubles are light and spacious, with high ceilings and tall windows. Rooms facing the inner courtyard are especially quiet.

D Hotel-Pension Elba, Bleibtreustr. 26, **T** 88 17 504, **F** 88 04 59 55, http://members.aol.com/hotelelba *S-Bahn Savignyplatz. Map 4, E1, p250* Attractive both inside and out, Elba has a comfortable feel and a friendly, informal atmosphere. Sizes vary among the 16 rooms but high ceilings give the place an airy feel. The decor is largely modern but with occasional odd pieces of carving.

D Hotel-Pension Imperator, Meinekestr. 5, **T** 88 14 181, **F** 88 51 919. *U-Bahn Uhlandstr., U-Bahn Kurfürstendamm. Map 4, E2, p250* This second-floor hotel has excellent modern art, rugs, some original 1900 features and a very large dopey dog. It's a worn, homely place, informal and friendly. It's also about as central as you can be in Berlin's western side without paying a fortune.

D Pension Gudrun, Bleibtreustr. 17, **T** 88 16 462, **F** 88 37 476. *S-Bahn Savignyplatz. Map 4, E1, p250* This small pension (only four rooms) is deceptively spacious: a family would quite easily fit in one of the larger rooms. The place is given a cosy and homely atmosphere by old but never ostentatious furniture and the multi-lingual enthusiasm of its owner.

D-E City Pension Alexandra, Wielandstr. 32, **T** 88 12 107, **F** 88 57 78 18. *U-Bahn Adenauerplatz, S-Bahn Savignyplatz. Map 4, F1, p250* On the second and third floors of a quiet block in the same street as Pension Dittberner, the Alexandra has wooden floors and high ceilings but rather uninspiring decor. The breakfast room is light and inviting but some of the bedrooms look rather dated.

D-E Hotel am Park, Sophie-Charlotten-Str. 57-58, **T** 32 13 485, www.pension-ampark.de *U-Bahn Sophie-Charlotte-Platz. Map 5, G2, p252* For anyone wanting to stay in the tree-lined avenues of Charlottenburg, this is a small, friendly and good-value option facing a park. Some rooms have balconies but the interior design is a strangely eclectic and largely 70s and 80s mix.

D-E **Hotel Pension Columbus**, Meinekerstr. 5, **T/F** 88 15 061. *U-Bahn Uhlandstr., U-bahn Kurfürstendamm. Map 4, E2, p250* On the third floor of an old building very near the Kurfürstendamm, the Columbus has a laid-back quality. Quiet rooms, with a mix of old and new furniture, have views over courtyards with trees. A very German-looking breakfast room is the scene for a good breakfast including freshly baked rolls and 10 different types of tea.

D-E **Pension Kettler**, Bleibtreustr. 19, **T** 88 34 949, **F** 88 24 228, www.kurfuerstendamm.de *Map 4, E1, p250* This well looked after Bohemian treasure trove has been here since 1900 and its current owner since the 1970s. Over this time she's built up a large collection of interesting art which covers the corridor walls from floor to ceiling. The classy furniture and decoration appear to have changed very little in the hundred years of the hotel, but don't seem at all worn or decrepit. The "Toulouse Lautrec" room in particular seems to have come straight out of turn-of-the-century Montmartre. Breakfast is taken in the rooms.

D-E **Pension Peters**, Kantstr. 146, **T** 31 22 278, **F** 31 23 519, www.pension-peters-berlin.de *S-Bahn Savignyplatz. Map 4, D1, p250* Friendly and efficient with simple modern furniture, pine floors, colourful rugs and some good contemporary art, Pension Peters is a good, cheaper option near the Kurfürstendamm. The pension also has apartments for rent, two nearby, and eight near Hackescher Markt in Mitte, starting at €60 a night, without breakfast.

D-E **Pension Viola Nova**, Kantstr. 146, **T** 31 57 260, **F** 31 23 314, www.violanova.de *S-Bahn Savignyplatz. Map 4, D1, p250* The sunny, front reception area and breakfast room of this hotel doubles as an exhibition space. Rooms vary in size but are all quite comfortable. Without at least a smattering of German you might struggle, however.

E Pension Knessebeck, Knessebeckstr. 86, **T** 31 27 255, **F** 31 39 507. *U-Bahn Ernst-Reuter-Pl, S-Bahn Savignyplatz. Map 4, C1, p250* A pension with a hostel atmosphere, the Knessebeck is a friendly good-value option very close to the smart eateries and shops of Savignyplatz. 'En suite' rooms have box-showers rather perfunctorily placed in the corner, chairs can be a little wobbly and the big buffet breakfast is served in a red and green room, but for this price in this location you can't really complain.

E-F Hotel-Pension Cortina, Kantstr. 140, **T** 31 39 059, **F** 31 27 396. *S-Bahn Savignyplatz. Map 4, D1 p250* When you are told by the talkative owner "If you want your feet kissed, go somewhere else", she means it. What you see is what you get here, the only frill being the "opulant" buffet breakfast. A shower in the room means a rather claustrophobic version of a phone box, and furniture is old without being antique. It's also very friendly, however.

Kreuzberg

Hotels and pensions

E Pension Kreuzberg, Grossbeerenstr. 64, **T** 25 11 362, **F** 25 10 638, www.pension-kreuzberg.de *U-Bahn Mehringdamm. Map 4, G11, p251* Thirteen large, simple rooms are the result of two floors of dark stairs. There's no lift and none of the rooms are en suite, but it's a welcoming place and if you want hostel prices without the frills or the hostellers, this could be a reasonable option.

F Die Fabrik, Schlesische Str. 18, **T** 61 17 116, **F** 61 82 974. *U-Bahn Schlesisches Tor. Map 3, F10, p249* A conversion of an old factory, Fabrik has a rather worn minimalist industrial stylishness, but one without much in the way of frills. Service is brisk and rooms (dorms, singles, doubles and triples) are decidedly basic.

Hostels

E Hotel Transit, Hagelbergerstr. 53-54, **T** 78 90 470, **F** 78 90 47 77, www.hotel-transit.de *U-Bahn Mehringdamm. Map 4, H12, p251* Most definitely a hostel, despite its name, Transit (sibling but not twin of Transit Loft, in Prenzlauerberg) is in an attractive old building and all rooms face a quiet inner courtyard. Rooms, ranging from single to six bed, are basic but all have en suite bathrooms. The breakfast buffet is excellent and continues until noon. Service is friendly and helpful, and although Kreuzberg is no longer the heart of Berlin's action, there are some good restaurants, cafés and bars around.

Potsdam

Hotels and pensions

B-C Das Kleine Apartmenthotel, Kurfürstenstr. 15, **T** 0331 27 91 10, **F** 0331 27 91 11, www.hollaenderhaus.potsdam.de *S-Bahn Potsdam Hbf Map 8, p256* On a relatively busy street on the northern edge of Potsdam's most interesting area, the Holländisches Viertel (Dutch Quarter), these hyper-modern apartments are kitted out with ample working space for business guests, but are also great places to stay for short-term visitors. From modern textiles and sofas to hi-fi and TVs that roll along runners on the ceiling, enabling them to be positioned at different points in the room, the design is high-tech, but also comfortable, with wooden floors, small kitchens and well-lit bathrooms.

C Hotel am Luisenplatz, Luisenplatz 5, **T** 0331 971 900, **F** 0331 971 90 19, www.hotel-luisenplatz.de *S-Bahn Potsdam Hbf Map 8, p256* As the name suggests, this hotel sits right on Luisenplatz, the town's focal (though not quite central) point. From rooms at the front you can look across the square at Potsdam's Brandenburg Gate and the main street of Brandenburger Strasse beyond. The interior is burgundy carpets and mahogany furniture and 11 suites have balconies and small kitchens. Ask about special rates for 'active weekends' and a 'midweek golf arrangement'. The newly opened **Bed and Breakfast am Luisenplatz** around the corner in the aptly named Zimmerstrasse is essentially a cheaper (**E**) and more modern annexe of the hotel.

D **Altstadt Potsdam**, Dortustr. 9/10, **T** 0331 28 49 90, **F** 0331 28 49 930, www.hotel-altstadt-potsdam.de *S-Bahn Potsdam Hbf. Map 8, p256* In the centre of Potsdam's old cobbled centre, this sturdy and handsome old building has 29 rooms and, judging by the visitors' book, plenty of satisfied customers. The decor is standard modern hotelesque but it's friendly and just off the main street, Brandenburger Strasse.

Köpenick

Hotels and pensions

D **Hotel Alter Markt**, Alter Markt 11a, **T** 65 57 386, **F** 65 57 388, www.berlin-info.de/hotel-alter-markt *S-Bahn Köpenick. Map 8, p256* If you're keen to stay outside of central Berlin, this
is quite a reasonable option. In the middle of the old cobbled centre of Köpenick, the Hotel Alter Markt has modern rooms facing the Heimatmuseum and an old square. Staff are friendly and there's a buffet breakfast. However, it's a fair walk or a tram ride from the station, and at the front of the hotel the sound of cars driving over the cobbles is noticeable.

Eating and drinking

In no other German city can you eat as well as in Berlin. Nowhere else is the restaurant scene so encouraged. Everything from pheasant breast garnished with truffles to the must-have-at-least-once Curry Wurst is offered. Berliners are also offered a whole host of entertainment including bars, pubs, cafés, wine bars, lounges, clubs and, for late-night munchies, an *Imbiss* – a kiosk selling drinks and light snacks.

The range of restaurants includes Indian, Greek, Japanese, Thai, modern European, Turkish and, of course, traditional German. Recently there have been more nouvelle cuisine restaurants opening up, exploring for example South African cooking.

Restaurants specializing in local dishes tend to serve fairly generous portions of heavy but tasty food. There are now many restaurants that maintain high European standards of international cuisine and, although often quite pricey, they are on the whole very good value for money, usually offering a fixed price menu at lunchtimes.

€

Price

Eating codes

€€€	26-40
€€	16-25
€	5-15

Prices refer to a main course with a glass of wine or beer .
A minimum service of 5% is expected.

In former West Berlin the most popular restaurants are clustered around Savignyplatz. The largest concentration of restaurants is in Mitte, or in former East Berlin, around Oranienburgerstrasse. The recently popular eating and drinking spots with young people are Prenzlauerberg, near Helmholzplatz, and Friedrichshain along Simon-Dach-Strasse. Kreuzberg is also very popular especially around Oranienstrasse where the restaurants are very busy.

Berlin is noted for its delicious and filling breakfasts. Most cafés serve a plate of cold meats and cheeses. Smoked salmon with horseradish is a favourite and highly recommended. Croissants are also popular as well as muesli and yogurt. At the weekend, brunch has become quite an institution. Priced at €6 upwards it normally includes bread, cheeses, hams, eggs, preserves, cereal and cold potato or pasta salad. Sometimes there will be sausages and bacon or grilled Mediterranean vegetables. Croissants and fruit are also normally served. Lunch is a simple affair. Most restaurants have a fixed menu which is usually economical and doesn't scrimp on the tastiness of the evening meal. These normally comprise of white meat such as veal and seasonal vegetables. Dinner is more of a substantial occasion. Fixed price menus are offered as well as *à la carte*. On the whole a main course of meat such as pork or schnitzel of pig's knuckle is typical. Seasonal vegetables are offered.

Where no closing time is given the venue stays open until the last guest leaves, whether this is at 2300 or 0200.

Mitte

Restaurants

€€€ Borchardt, Französischestr. 47, **T** 20 38 71 10. *U-Bahn Französische Str. Daily 1100-0100. Map 7, F6, p254* Next to the Süddeutsche Zeitung office, this restaurant serving international cuisine is favoured by politicians and journalists from across the spectrum. It was their favourite on the night of the 2002 election. The interior is the original dating from the18th century and the marble columns, mosaics and period-style floors make this Gendarmenmarkt institution well worth a visit. The food, such as trout with asparagus or roast duck with cabbage, is first rate.

€€€ **Dachgarten Restaurant Käfer am Bundestag**, the Reichstag, Platz der Republik, **T** 22 62 99 33. *U-Bahn Unter den Linden. Daily 0900-1700, 1830-2400. Map 7, E1, p254* The location of this restaurant at the top of the Reichstag is impressive, but sadly, the food is not. Having your dinner opposite Sir Norman Foster's dome overlooking the city is great fun but the food is not great and it's overpriced. A reservation is recommended and also helps you skip the queue as you can take the entrance on the right- hand side normally reserved for disabled people.

€€€ **Lutter und Wegner**, Charlottenstr. 56, **T** 202 94 40, www.lutter-wegner-gendarmenmarkt.de *U-Bahn Französische Str. Daily 1100-0200. Map 7, H6, p254* The fact that the 18th-century romantic writer ETA Hoffmann, author of *The Nutcracker*, used to frequent this rather grand oak-panelled restaurant may be what first attracts you but the extensive wine list and succulent, reasonably priced Austrian and German food is what will entice you to return. In the summer months smart tables spill out onto the pavement and year round the dark, antiquated *Wein Stube*

★ **Berlinesque meals**

Best

- Kartoffelsuppe (potato soup)
- Eisbein mit Pfifferlingen und Kraut (braised pork knuckle on a bed of wild mushrooms and cabbage)
- Eierpfannkuchen mit Apfelsauce (egg-based pancakes with apple sauce)
- A Berliner Weisse mit Schuss (a sweet beer mixed with either raspberry or woodruff cordial)

(wine room) complete with Cuban cigars can be found next door. The food is unpretentious and impressive although some things like the salads could be made a bit more exciting. The menu changes daily and can be viewed on the website.

€€€ **McBride's**, Oranienburgerstr. 32, **T** 28 38 64 61. *U-Bahn Oranienburger Tor, S-Bahn Oranienburger Str. 1130-0100. Map 7, B6, p254* Beautifully situated in the restored Heckmann courtyards this restaurant is a delightful place to eat especially in the summer when the conservatory and the garden can be used. The food is simple but good – asparagus, quiche, salad and soup. The ample pork roast on Sundays is very Germanic and succulent. The wines are excellent. Service can be slow.

€€€ **Schwarzenraben**, Neue Schönhauser Str. 13, **T** 28 39 16 98, www.schwarzenraben.de *S-Bahn Hackescher Markt, U-Bahn Weinmeisterstr. Daily 1000-2400. Map 7, B9, p255* The Schwarzenraben has come under quite a lot of controversy recently due to the dichotomy of its altruistic past and its commercial present. The building in the German neo-renaissance style was originally a soup kitchen for the poor but has now been transformed into a rather fashionable bar with an excellent restaurant at the back, open only in the evenings.

The food is superb, for example the grilled vegetables or tuna with a tomato and olive salsa, and the service is impeccable. There is a small garden open in summer and an Asian food counter in the bar during the week. Highly recommended.

€€ **Hackescher Hof**, Rosenthaler Str. 40/41, **T** 283 52 93, www.hackescher-hof.de *S-Bahn Hackescher Markt. Mon-Fri 0700-0300, Sat and Sun 0900-0300. Map 7, B9, p255* However popular this may have been, the bistro situated in the Hackeschen Höfe complex has rather lost its edge, since filling up with out-of-towners whilst the locals head to the Schwarzenraben down the road. However, for quite a while, it was *the* place to go for the glam, the intellectuals, the young and the old. And, to its credit is still usually filled with Berliners as well as tourists. The food is fairly priced and uncomplicated and for lunch there are reasonable fixed price menus. Breakfast is served till 1400.

€€ **Taba**, Torstra. 164, **T** 28 04 09 60. *U-Bahn Rosenthaler Platz. Daily from 1900. Map 2, F5, p246* Taba is one of the oldest Brazilian restaurants in the city and on Sundays is the Brazil meeting- place because *Pagode* (music and dance typical of the Bahian region) is played. On Wednesdays and Thursdays there is a buffet of delicious specialties such as *feijoada* (black beans), *moqueca* (Bahian-style fish stew) and grilled meats. The restaurant is actually owned by a Turk which made the location quite hostile ground during the Turkey-Brazil semi final of the 2002 World Cup.

€€ XII Apostel, Georgenstr. 2, **T** 201 02 22. *S-Bahn and U-Bahn Friedrichstr. Daily 24 hours. Map 7, D4, p254* Once you step through the thick, red velvet curtain you will feel as if you are no longer in Berlin. Perfect for late-night dining and built under the arches of an S-Bahn railway bridge with juddering, but beautifully decorated Michelangelo-style ceilings, this large but intimate, restaurant serves oversized and delicious wood oven-cooked pizzas. Unlimited amount of pizza for the price of one on Mondays.

● *XII Apostel's little sister restaurant is at Bleibtreustr. 49 by Savignyplatz S-Bahn.*

€€ Yosoy, Rosenthaler Str. 37, **T** 28 39 12 13. *S-Bahn Hackescher Markt, U-Bahn Weinmeisterstr. Daily from 1100. Map 7, B9, p255* The feeling that you're in a North African souk is all pervasive when visiting this late-night haunt. Bottles of red wine seem to be consumed by the gallon while the delicious tapas are served on tiled counters. It is very pleasant and laid-back amongst the super smart Mitte bars.

€€ Zum Nussbaum, Am Nussbaum 3, **T** 242 30 95. *S-Bahn and U-Bahn Alexanderplatz. Daily from 1200. Map 7, F10, p255* This restaurant in one of the alleys off the Nikolaiviertel and as an inn is one of the best known in town. The building is a reconstruction of the original 16th-century inn and its menu offers traditional Berlin food. If you fancy pig's knuckle and rolled, pickled herrings this is the place to go. In the summer you can sit in the small pretty garden. Popular with tourists.

€ Monsieur Vuong, Alte Schönhauser Str. 46, **T** 30 87 26 43, www.monsieurvuong.de *U-Bahn Rosa Luxemburg Platz. Mon-Sat 1200-2400, Sun 1400-0200. Map 7, A10, p255* Monsieur Vuong has the much sought-after ability of not only attracting a cluster of prominent Berliners normally from the media and arts, but also drawing the regular young street crowd. And at €6.50 for the

Indochinese menu it's no wonder why. Rumour has it that the portions have become smaller but the food's so good you'll want to come back anyway. Notice the blown-up photo of a very good-looking young Asian sailor on the wall. This is Monsieur Vuong himself, now in his 70s.

€ **Surf and Sushi**, Oranienburger Str. 17, **T** 28 38 48 98, www.surfandsushi.de *S-Bahn Hackescher Markt. Mon-Fri 1200-2400, Sat and Sun 1300-2400. Map 7, C8, p255* Served by an army of men and women all in black but with seemingly only one chef this conveniently located sushi and internet café remains popular, probably due to the fact that on Monday, Wednesday and Friday Happy Hour lasts all day. The sushi ranges from €2.15 to 15 and is tasty but sometimes a little too dry. The internet is expensive at €2.15 for half an hour. Deliveries are also available.

Cafés

Barcomi's Deli, Sophienstr. 21, 2nd Courtyard, **T** 28 59 83 63. *S-Bahn Hackescher Markt, U-Bahn Weinmeisterstr. Mon-Sat 0900-2200, Sun 1000-2200. Map 7, B8, p255* The spacious and light bar in this intimate courtyard along with its 13 home-roasted coffees and the absolutely delectable cakes on offer is a big temptation. The raspberry chocolate cake, carrot cake and New York cheese cake are just a few. The offer of a choice of four for €4 is highly recommended. The delicious bagels with home-made cream cheese and the wide variety of teas are also impressive.

Cinema Café, Rosenthaler Str. 39, **T** 280 64 15. *S-Bahn Hackescher Markt, U-Bahn Weinmeisterstr. Daily 1200-0200. Map 7, B9, p255* This tiny café with its walls festooned with film accessories has managed to survive 40 years of socialism as well as 10 years of capitalism. It's noted for always having good-looking girls smoking and drinking coffee. Packed in the evening.

Night owls specials

- XII Apostel, p145
- Yosoy, p145
- Schwarzes Café, p155
- Schwarz-Sauer, p153

Galao A Pastelaria, Weinbergsweg 8 (beginning of Kastanien-allee), **T** 44 04 68 82. *U-Bahn Rosenthaler Platz. Mon-Fri 0800-1900, Sat and Sun 1000-1800. Map 2, F6, p246* The best coffee in Berlin. The pastelaria also offers tasty pastries such as Portuguese croissants and cakes. Home-made soups and pasta with meat are also available. The relaxed ambience and the cushions lazily thrown on the steps outside assure this is a favourite among students.

Gorki Park, Weinbergsweg 25 (beginning of Kastanienallee), **T** 448 72 86. *U-Bahn Rosenthaler Platz. Daily 1000-0200. Map 2, F6, p246* Gorki Park is very well situated between Mitte and Prenz-lauerberg to draw both crowds before a night out. Alternatively you could just stay here enjoying the newspapers and the tempting Russian zakuski (canapes) which range from piroshki to aubergine caviar and sour pickles.

Kapelle, Zionskirchstr. 22-24, **T** 44 34 13 00, www.cafe-kapelle.de *U-Bahn Rosenthaler Platz. Daily 0900-0300. Map 2, E6, p246* Kapelle, with its view onto the Zionskirche, has quite a history as it was here the Red Orchestra Resistance Group (they helped Jews escape before the Soviets accidentally blew their cover) met during the Nazi era. It serves very tasty breakfasts and light snacks such as bagels and fresh soup. When in season the pumpkin soup is always very popular. It is also in a good location to catch all the Sunday flea market shoppers at Arkonaplatz.

Eating and drinking

Marcann's, Invalidenstr. 112, **T** 28 38 61 71. *U-Bahn Zinnowitzer Str. Mon-Fri 0700–1800, Sat 0830-1400. Map 2, G2, p246* A modern, airy café serving tasty paninis and good coffee. In the summer the iced coffees go down a treat.

Obst & Gemüse, Oranienburgerstr. 48/49, **T** 282 96 47. *U-Bahn Oranienburger Tor, S-Bahn Oranienburger Str. Mon-Fri from 0830, Sat and Sun from 0900. Map 7, B5, p254* Previously a fruit and veg shop, this trendy hang-out has a great view of the street through its floor-to-ceiling windows. In the summer there is seating on benches outside. Good coffee and bagels are served.

Strandbad Mitte, Kleine Hamburger Str. 16, **T** 283 68 77. *U-Bahn Rosenthaler Platz. Mon-Thu 0900–0120, Fri and Sat 0900-0230, Sun 1000–0130. Map 7, A7, p255* Confusingly designed with a wall of aquarium tanks but no fish in sight, this bar/café is a great place to get value-for-money food. The range of cocktails is pretty good. Strandbad Mitte is very popular in the summer and is well situated to see what's happening on the trendy Auguststrasse.

Suppenbörse, Dorotheenstr. 43, **T** 20 64 95 98. *S-Bahn and U-Bahn Friedrichstr. Mon-Fri 1000-1800, Sat 1200-1630. Map 7, E5, p254* The Suppenbörse is a great alternative to all the greasy, fast- food places in Friedrichstrasse station. The soup is cheap, very tasty and comes with as much bread as you want.

Telecafé, top of the Television Tower, Panoramastr. 1a, **T** 242 33 33, www.berlinerfernsehturm.de *S-Bahn and U-Bahn Alexanderplatz. Daily Mar-Oct 0900-0100, Nov-Feb 1000-2400. Map 7, D11, p255* With the best view of Berlin it's no surprise that the quality and value of the coffee and snacks leave quite a lot to be desired. However, it's a great place to start your trip and get your bearings.

Zosch, Tucholskystr. 30, **T** 280 76 64. *S-Bahn Oranienburger Str. Mon-Fri 1600-0200, Sat and Sun from 1200. Map 7, B6, p254* One of the first pub/cafés of the post-reunification time, Zosch is still doing well. It has become quite a popular local with inhabitants of the surrounding buildings, serving food upstairs and hosting live music in the bar downstairs. Fridays is usually a good ska and reggae night. There are tables outside in the summer.

Zucca, Am Zwirngraben 11/12, **T** 24 72 12 12. *S-Bahn Hackescher Markt. Mon-Fri from 0900, Sat and Sun from 1000. Map 7, C9, p255* Situated under the S-Bahn arches this classically chic-looking café is very large and grand-looking with chandeliers and mirrors from floor to ceiling. A lovely place to meet friends with a long, impressive bar to keep you occupied.

Tiergarten

Restaurants

€€ **Tony Roma's**, Marlene-Dietrich-Platz 3, **T** 25 29 58 30. *S-Bahn and U-Bahn Potsdamer Platz. Daily from 1130. Map 6, D4, p253* If you can overcome the over-the-top American interior design then the food here is not actually that bad. The house specialty is spare ribs at €12, which can't be too fattening as this diner is a favourite with the dancers over the road at *Cats*.

Cafés

Café am Neuen See, Lichtensteinallee 1, **T** 254 49 30. *S-Bahn Tiergarten. Daily Mar-Oct 1000-2400, daily Nov-Feb 1000-2000. Map 4, C5, p250* This beer garden in the middle of the Tiergarten where there are boats to rent has become a very popular summer hang-out. The food is Bavarian with Weisswurst (white sausages) going down well with a good Weissbier. There is a choice of two large, thin-crust Italian-style pizzas available in the self-service café. The candle-lit tables and tranquil lake make it very picturesque.

Prenzlauerberg

Restaurants

€€ **Frida Kahlo**, Lychener Str. 37, **T** 445 70 16, www.fridakahlo.de *U-Bahn Eberswalder Str. Daily from 1000. Map 2, C8, p247* Prints of the artist's work adorn the ochre and brown walls of this Mexican restaurant. However, the female equivalent of Salvador Dalí would turn in her grave if she saw the menu. The food is more Santa Monica than Mexican but, despite this geographical and culinary error, it is still lip-smacking. The pancakes at breakfast time can be delectable, depending on the cook, and the guacamole and fried chicken are always done well. The cocktails served between 1800 and 2100 are €4.90.

€€ **La Bodeguita del Medio**, Lychener Str. 6, **T** 442 96 98. *U-Bahn Eberswalder Str. Daily from 1800. Map 2, C8, p247* Named after the bar in Havana that Ernest Hemingway, Al Capone and Pablo Neruda used to frequent, this Cuban restaurant bar offers guacamole, beans, rice and tapas as well as intoxicating cocktails such as caipirinhas and mojitos. The salsa and *son* music also give this place a real Latin American feel.

€€ **Pasternak**, Knaackstr. 22-24, **T** 441 33 99, www.restaurant-pasternak.de *U-Bahn Senefelder Platz. Daily 1000-0200. Map 2, E9, p247* Here you can enjoy classics such as beef stroganoff but at a fairly inflated €14.90. The breakfasts are also expensive but worth it as there seems to be so much, and the garnishes, like horseradish, taste especially good. The Russian dishes are done well.

★ Banging breakfasts

Best

- •Restauration 1900, p151
- •November, p153
- •Pasternak, p150
- •Café Berio, p158

Speed of service leaves something to be desired. On Tuesday and Thursday there is live music that ranges from Russian songs from the 30s to the 60s, to Russian Swing and Folklore as well as yiddish favourites.

€€ **Restauration 1900**, Husemannstr. 1, **T** 442 24 94, www.restauration-1900.de *U-Bahn Eberswalder Str., U-Bahn Senefelder Platz. Daily from 0930 (summer) 1100-2400 (winter) Map 2, D9, p247* This restaurant is quite a local hang-out. Situated directly on Kollwitz Platz it is somewhere that attracts young and old Berliners alike. There is both international and German cuisine with some interesting touches such as caviar potatoes and turkey with mango sauce but many of the dishes are fairly straightforward and taste very good. At weekends a delicious and quite substantial brunch is served.

€ **Der Imbiss**, Kastanienallee 49. *Tram 13, 15, 50. Daily from 1800 till late depending on the owner's mood. Map 2, E7, p247* Despite having no name this *Imbiss* has proved extremely popular after its opening at the beginning of 2002. The owner, Gordon, an eccentric Canadian musician, has combined excellent quality food at cheap prices with an *Imbiss* size and casualness. The food is Southeast Asian and dishes such as tandoori fish cooked in something similar to a kiln must be tasted. The fruit cocktails are fantastic and superb for hangovers. Listen out for the Mongolian chanting or epic film soundtrack.

Eating and drinking

€ **Kommandantur Pizzeria**, Knaackstr. 18, **T** 44 03 14 68. *U-Bahn Senefelder Platz. Daily from 1600. Map 2, E9, p247* This is a standard pizzeria in an old-fashioned Italian tavern that offers above average food at a standard price. Its location opposite the Wasserturm (Water Tower), which some consider to be the heart of Prenzlauerberg, makes it more notable than most pizza parlours.

€ **Schulter Junge**, corner of Lychener Str. and Danziger Str. *U-Bahn Eberswalder Str. Map 2, C8, p247* This restaurant is more like a real German *kneipe* or pub. Don't be alarmed by the strange looks that you get as you walk through the door but simply go through and sit down at one of the tables in the back. The food is typically German and delicious with generous, inexpensive portions and friendly service. The schnitzel and eierpfannkuchen (pancakes) with apple sauce must be tried.

€ **Thüringer Stuben**, Stargarder Str. 28, **T** 446 33 39. *S-Bahn Prenzlauer Allee. Mon-Sat 1600-0100. Map 2, C10, p247* If wood wainscoting and heavy meat cooking are your thing then this is the place to go. The menu offers specialties from Thüring (a region in the middle of Germany renowned for its food), such as the famous Bratwurst (fried sausage) or the more delicate lamb fillets with garlic and beetroot salad. Very good traditional German food.

€ **Voland**, Wichertstr. 63, **T** 444 04 22, www.voland-café.de *S-Bahn and U-Bahn Schönhauser Allee. Daily from 1800. Map 2, B9, p247* It is easy to see the inspiration for this restaurant. If the name doesn't give it away then the pictures inside should – all illustrations of Bulgakov's masterpiece *The Master and Margarita*. The locals, however, are not only concerned with literature (readings regularly take place here, as well as live music) but also with peasant-like Russian food. The fact that most of the voices heard are Russian gives the food a good recommendation.

Cafés

An einem Sonntag im August, Kastanienallee 103, **T** 44 05 12 28, www.erotisches-zur-nacht.de *U-Bahn Eberswalder Str. Daily from 0900. Map 2, D7, p247* This local, situated in the heart of Prenzlauerberg, is popular for its buffet of bread, eggs, cheese and wurst, priced at €3 and served from 0900. The café regularly hosts readings of erotic poetry. Check the website for more details.

November, Husemannstr. 15, **T** 442 84 25. *U-Bahn Senefelderplatz. Mon-Thu 1000-0200, Fri 1000-0300, Sat 0900-0300, Sun 0900-0200. Map 2, D9, p247* This café is famous for allowing visitors to make their own waffles at the luscious Sunday brunch which costs €7.50. It is on a quiet, tree-lined street and offers good quality food and drinks at all other times as well.

Schwarz-Sauer, Kastanienallee 13, T 448 56 33. *U-Bahn Eberswalder Str. Daily 0800-0600. Map 2, D7, p247* Schwarz-Sauer is very well situated on this trendy street full of young, arty, eccentric and alternative types and it's even better when the tables outside are set up. Always packed, you will inevitably bump into friends, and you can keep an eye on what's going on in hip and happening Prenzlauerberg. The bar serves cocktails and beers and sushi is also offered. A great atmosphere.

Titanic, Christburgerstr. 36, **T** 442 03 40. *Tram 2, 3, 4, 20. Daily from 1000. Map 2, E10, p247* The attractive, ivy-clad building on the corner of Winsstrasse and Christburgerstrasse houses a neighbourly café where the breakfasts are very good and generous on Sundays when there is an impressive buffet on offer. You should come early to get a place as the service is uneven depending on the staff. When the weather is good there are tables outside.

★ **Best**

Picturesque cafés

•Zum Nussbaum, p145
•Café am Neuen See, p149
•Café Schönbrunn, p154

Friedrichshain

Restaurants

€€ **Sud – Vino e Cucina Mediterranea**, Hufelandstr. 21,
T 42 80 18 46. *Tram 2,3,4. Mon-Sat 1200-2300. Map 2, F11, p247*
Simple and chic, this Italian restaurant offers above average food
such as its fish specialties and freshly made pasta. The tables
outside in the summer are great to people-watch and the house
wine, made ecologically in Lazio, is recommended.

€ **Lola**, Kopernikusstr. 3, **T** 29 66 70 28, www.r-w-b.de/
puertalatina/lola *S-Bahn and U-Bahn Warschauer Str., Tram
20. Mon-Sat from 1700, Sun from 1000. Map 3, C11, p249* In
this genial and stress-free Spanish restaurant/bar you really get
a taste of Iberian life. The tapas and wine choice are excellent and
on Thursdays and Sundays after 2000 original Spanish videos are
shown, free of charge, in an adjoining room. The calamares salad
is very tasty and the mixed plate of starters to share is good value
for money.

Cafés

Café Schönbrunn, Volkspark Friedrichshain, **T** 42 02 81 91. *Bus
200. This café in the park is not so easy to find but if you follow the*

Käthe-Nieder-Kirchnerstr. where it goes into the green then you're nearly there.   Mon-Fri 1100-0100, Sat and Sun 1000-0200. Map 2, G11, p247   The café with its glass windows and largish seating area outside offers great views of the park and the lake. In the day it is more of a meeting place for walkers but at night it turns into more of a lounge. During the Love Parade (see p190) it is the location of the infamous 60-hour party.

Charlottenburg

Restaurants

€€ **Florian**, Grolmannstr. 52, **T** 31 39 184. *S-Bahn Savignyplatz. Daily 1800-0300. Map 4, D1, p250* A solid German restaurant with natural style, class and an almost 20-year-long tradition. After 2300, when they start to serve their bratwurst (fried sausage) with sauerkraut (best order 10 pieces, they are very small and very delicious), Florian turns into an inspired artists' boozer.

Cafés

Café Hardenberg, Hardenbergstr. 10, T 312 26 44. *U-Bahn Ernst-Reuter-Platz. Sun-Thu 0900-0100, Fri and Sat 0900-0200. Map 4, D2, p250* This spacious comfortable café, situated opposite the Technical University, is ironically always packed with arty students ploughing over their books. The Milchkaffees are yummy and can be chatted over for hours and the light food and snacks available such as potato cake or apple strudel are good at reasonable prices.

Schwarzes Café, Kantstr. 148, **T** 313 80 38. *S-Bahn and U-Bahn Savignyplatz. Open 24 hours Mon, Wed-Sun. Map 5, H6, p252* Schwarzes Café has always been an institution among the cafés in Berlin since it opened in 1978. The black-tiled toilets with

★ **German-style restaurants**

Best

- •Schulter Junge, p152
- •Lutter und Wegner, p142
- •Zur Henne, p156

windows in the walls make calls of nature that bit more exciting!
Serving breakfasts and drinks around the clock except for Tuesday
mornings when it is shut for an hour, it has become something of
a lifesaver for night owls.

Kreuzberg

Restaurants

€ **Fish 'n' Chips**, Yorckstr.15. *U-Bahn Mehringdamm, U-Bahn
Möckernbrücke. Mon-Fri 1200-2400, Sat and Sun 1400-2400. Map
4, G11, p251* Reputedly the only *Imbiss* in Berlin where you can
get proper British fish and chips. At least that's what they think.
The fish and chips are quite good but not quite in the style we
get in Britain and there's not a newspaper in sight. Still, they're
pretty tasty and you can also buy Heinz Baked Beans and Marmite.
The enormous bellied grumpy owner could, however, be straight
out of your local chippie.

€ **Zur Henne**, Leuschnerdamm 25, **T** 614 77 30. *U-Bahn
Kottbusser Tor. Wed-Sun from 1900. Map 3, E5, p248* This
traditional restaurant on the banks of the Spree is home to not
only the best chicken in town but also to one of the most notable
"relics" of a bygone age. Behind the bar there is a letter from
President JF Kennedy apologizing for not visiting the restaurant

on his 1961 visit to Berlin. The menu is half a roast chicken with either potato salad or sauerkraut and costs €6. The sauerkraut is recommended. There is no cutlery for the chicken – just eat it with your fingers. One of the best atmospheres in town.

Cafés

Bateau Ivre, Oranienstr. 18, **T** 61 40 36 59. *U-Bahn Görlitzer Bahnhof. Sun-Thu from 0900. Map 3, E4, p248* A lovely, laid-back place that even by its name (drunken ship) inspires a relaxed and friendly atmosphere. Good coffee as well as good food and the big glass windows make for great viewing of all the eccentrics on Oranienstrasse. What more could you want from a café?

Café Adler, Friedrichstr. 206, **T** 251 89 65. *U-Bahn Kochstr. Mon-Sat 0930-2400, Sun 0930-1900. Map 6, C8, p253* Situated in protected buildings this café was around when the Berlin Wall was standing. The back room is extremely soporific and is one of the only places in Berlin that is no smoking. The service has become better but the cakes are still quite dry. Very popular with tourists wanting to see where Checkpoint Charlie stood and where everyone used to have their first western coffee when they had just left the east.

Schöneberg

Restaurants

€€ Pranzo e Cena, Goltzstr. 32, **T** 216 35 14. *U-Bahn Nollendorfplatz, U-Bahn Eisenacher Str. Daily 1200-2400. Map 4, H6, p250* With a fairly simple camel-and-creamy-yellow interior and no excessive frills this restaurant has managed to overcome the curse of this corner where many other establishments have opened and closed within months. Pranzo e Cena offers uncomplicated and very good Italian food, such as home-made ravioli parcels. A lunch menu costs €7.50, the evening menu, €12.

Cafés

Café Berio, Massenstr. 7, **T** 216 19 46, www.berio.de *U-Bahn Nollendorfplatz. Daily 0800-0100. Map 4, G7, p251* Always packed, this café in the very gay area of Nollendorfplatz, serves fantastic cakes and coffee. The breakfasts are delicious and as well as the traditional German kind there is also the possibility of French toast and American dishes. The milkshakes also deserve a mention. Make sure you know your gender symbols for a safe trip to the loo.

Café M, Goltzstr. 33, **T** 216 70 92. *U-Bahn Eisenacher Str., U-Bahn Nollendorfplatz. Mon-Fri 0800-0200, Sat 0900-0300, Sun 0900-0200. Map 4, H6, p250* This extremely cool bar/café has existed since the early 80s and has always been the perfect place to watch the young, cool yet upwardly mobile, of the big city go by whilst sipping scrumptious coffee. The electric disco music adds to the very contemporary Berlin atmosphere.

Neukölln

Cafés

Café Xenzi, Selchower Str. 31, **T** 622 39 29. *Daily 0900-0100. U-Bahn Boddinstr.* Best in the summer when you're invited to sit outside and indulge in an open-air coffee or hot chocolate with extra milk. The service is friendly and the breakfasts range from sweet cakes at €2.30 to smoked salmon at €5.80. A favourite is one of the rich tortes accompanied by an indulgent mini hot chocolate.

Berlin offers some of the best nightlife in Europe (see also music venues, p180). There is a very laid-back vibe which make this city so accessible yet, at the same time, everywhere you go the clientele seem incredibly cutting edge making you think you've stumbled upon an undiscovered underground spot. Since the Wall came down former East Berlin has turned into one of the most sought-after locations with trendy bars and restaurants springing up everywhere. The further east you go the more engaging the bars, cafés and restaurants tend to be. The further west you go the smarter and more elegant the bars are. All are dark and retro, each with the obligatory DJ who spins electric ballroom lounge grooves.

The club scene is much bigger than just the outdated stereotype of Germans and techno. There are amazing venues attracting top performers, be it LTJ Bukem at Club Casino or Bob Dylan at the Columbia Halle; whatever you're into, you're sure to find it in Berlin. Bars usually open at 2200 and then close when the last guest leaves. Take this as a rule unless

otherwise specified.

Berlin is also host to **Geheimtip parties**. These 'secret tip' parties are a part of the Berlin East-side nightlife. You have to be in the know, which normally means residency or the right people, but if you are lucky you might discover the venues for favourites, such as the **Mittwochclub**, every Wednesday. Sometimes the venue is only known moments before party time. Regular features of geheimtips are climbing down trap doors into the depths of Berlin, dancing to electric funk and salsa DJs, fussball tables, long drinks, absinthe and emerging back onto the streets as the sun is well past risen.

Mitte

Bars

Bar Deutschlands, Dorotheenstr. 65. *S-Bahn and U-Bahn Friedrichstr., S-Bahn Unter den Linden. 1000-2300. Map 7, E4, p254* Known to be the best-protected bar in any capital, Bar Deutschlands is situated right behind the US Embassy, which has been surrounded by a tank and 8-10 police armed with machine guns since September 11 2001. Fortunately, it is now possible to visit the bar without several forms of identification.

Bergstüb'l, Veteranenstr. 25. *U-Bahn Rosenthaler Platz, Tram 6, 8, 50. Daily from 1600. Map 2, E6, p246* Always packed and very popular among the young, cool crowd of Mitte and Prenzlauerberg, this laid-back bar with the Berlin must-have of its own live DJ, is a great spot. The crowd is into the whole Berlin retro look of 70s' pinks and browns, and the comfy sixth-form-common-room-esque chairs make it a place to stay all night. There are always a few lively characters as well as a few shady ones!

Erdbeer-Bar, Max-Beer-Str. 56. *U-Bahn Rosa-Luxemburg-Platz. Daily from 1800. Map 7, A11, p255* Everything in this extremely trendy bar is decorated in red and with an interior that is straight out of a second-hand 70s' shop. The music from the house DJ is always electric disco and the atmosphere is very funky. You may have trouble meeting friends here as it's almost too dark to see properly, but in spite of this, it's where everybody meets before a night out, or even just to stay and drink cheap beers and good cocktails (€4-10). The best strawberry daiquiri in Berlin. This bar is highly recommended.

Goldrausch, corner of Rosenthaler Str. and Torstr., **T** 28 09 39 09, www.goldrausch.info *U-Bahn Rosenthaler Platz. Daily from 1800. Map 2, F6, p246* The former Burger King restaurant is now a plush bar split over two levels of kitsch gold and red. The atmosphere is very gay but anything goes so don't be put off, although you may be after seeing the price list.

Greenwich, Gipsstr. 5, **T** 0177 280 88 06. *U-Bahn Weinmeisterstr. Daily 1900-0600. Map 7, A8, p255* Although one of Mitte's fashionable bars you get the impression that Greenwich (pronounced Green Vitch) has somehow passed its sell-by date. Still highly chic-looking with elegant decor, but the cocktail list leaves you wanting more and the music hasn't caught up with the electro lounge style of other bars and instead just sounds like noise.

Hotelbar, Zionskirchestr. 5, **T** 44 32 85 77, www.hotelbar-berlin.de *U-Bahn Bernauer Str. Wed-Sat from 2200. Map 2, E7, p247* A 70s-style bar with an orange colour theme, this new kid on the Mitte block has already made itself quite well known and well liked by having cracking music from new artists and promoting the bungalow record label (www.bungalow.de). The interior is retrograde but not too original and there is a nice-sized dance space at the back giving it more of a clubby feeling. Entry price varies but is never too expensive.

Newton Bar, Charlottenstr. 57, **T** 20 61 29 99, www.newton-bar.de
U-Bahn Französische Str. Daily 1000-0300. Map 7, G5, p254 With
an entire humidor room upstairs, it's almost compulsory to smoke
a cigar while stretching back in the heavy, red-leather armchairs
and gazing at one of Helmut Newton's most famous photographs,
which is the largest in private ownership. The clientele is beautiful,
but quite snooty, and Peter Ustinov is rumoured to visit whenever
he's in town. Next door an *Edelimbiss* (literally a noble *Imbiss*) has
been set up and over the road is the restaurant Lutter und Wegner,
see p142. Expensive (cocktails €8-14).

Seven Lounge, Ackerstr. 20, **T** 27 59 69 79, www.seven-lounge.de
U-Bahn Rosenthaler Platz. Daily from 1800. Map 2, F5, p246
The generic Mitte bar, which holds claim to weird and wonderful
lighting, weird in that it can break easily causing some painful
injuries, so watch your head. The man behind this bar is clearly a
fan of the 60s' B-Movie, with the interior straight out of a science
fiction film. There is a dimly lit private room at the back and the
cocktails are fairly priced (€5-9).

Strandbar am Spree, in Monbijouplatz between Oranienburgerstr. and Monbijoustr. *S-Bahn Hackescher Markt. Map 7, C7,
p255* This bar/café in the middle of the park provides the much
sought-after perfect summer atmosphere. Only open during the
summer months, it has deckchairs set out and sand to give it the
right vibe. A lovely place to while away the summer days.

Tacheles, Oranienburgerstr. 54-56. *U-Bahn Oranienburger Tor,
S-Bahn Oranienburger Str. Map 7, B5, p254* This bar on the fifth
floor of an artist commune has a certain sixth-form common
room and anarchists' squat feel to it. With a wall missing so you
can look over Berlin and a bar that looks like a temporary set up
at a mate's party, this is a definite must see. Try and stay for the
cine-reel projections late into the night.

Clubs

Acud, Veteranenstr. 21, **T** 449 10 67, www.acud.de *U-Bahn Rosenthaler Platz, Tram 6, 8, 50. Daily from 2100. Map 2, E6, p246* This culture centre is almost too good to be true. The shabby and almost dilapidated location is host to a theatre, cinema, club, café, gallery and music venue. There are regular concerts from drum 'n' bass to reggae, funk and jazz. For the more inspired there are open mike nights from Sunday to Thursday. The future of the centre is perpetually in question because of financial issues. The website is very interesting for all aspects of *Acud* including its history.

Cookies, Charlottenstr. 44. *S-Bahn and U-Bahn Friedrichstr. Tue and Thu from 2300, first Sat of each month from 2300. Map 7, E5, p254* Even shaking off its location-ever-changing illegal former self and settling down in Charlottenstrasse in Mitte hasn't shelved Cookies' trendy crowd. Every Tuesday and Thursday this is where the fashion-conscious of Berlin swarm in order to dance to minimalist house or electric funk in the ballroom-like club. There is a bar in what was a vault downstairs and the unisex loos are quite a shocker, especially towards the end of the evening. The club is considered such a Berlin icon that it was used in the film *Lotus Style*, the recent winner of the Sehnsüchte short film festival.

Grüner Salon, Rosa-Luxemburg-Platz 2, **T** 28 59 89 36, www.gruener-salon.de *U-Bahn Rosa-Luxemburg-Platz. Check the website for opening hours and programme. Map 7, A11, p255* Decorated forest green as one would expect from the name and identical in appearance, save the colour, to its sister club, the Roter Salon (see below), the Grüner Salon is one of the most pleasant clubs in Berlin. It has a regular programme keeping Friday as a funk night where they play proper old school funk and soul. Lots of Aretha! There are swing and tango classes and events, as well as frequent live shows. It's also here that n-tv talkshows are produced.

Roter Salon an der Volksbühne, Rosa-Luxemburg-Platz 2, **T** 24 06 58 06, www.roter-salon.de *U-Bahn Rosa-Luxemburg-Platz. Check the website for opening hours and DJ line-up. Map 7, A11, p255* Situated around the other side of the Volksbühne complex from the Grüner Salon, the Roter Salon hosts evenings more geared to young Mitte clubbers with acts ranging from French House to the indie pop Karrera Klub. It is also a venue for live concerts and for readings. The plush, red-leather sofas create a decadent atmosphere. Regular tango night on Wednesdays.

Sage Club, Köpenicker Str. 78, **T** 27 59 10 82, www.sage-club.de *Thu from 2200 , Fri-Sun 2300-0900. U-Bahn Heinrich-Heine-Str. Map 3, C5, p248* Quite an ostentatious atmosphere, but still a great place to go, even just to see the fire-breathing dragon sculpture over the dance floor and the swimming pool outside in the summer. There is a rather strict door policy but the least pretentious nights are Friday when the music is funk and Sunday when it's garage and techno.

! The U-Bahn station Rosa-Luxemburg-Platz has had six changes in name since it opened in 1913, all made on political grounds.

Prenzlauerberg

Bars

Bar 23, Lychener Str. 23, www.bar23.de *U-Bahn Eberswalder Str. Daily from 1900. Check the website for the music line-up. Map 2, C8, p247* The only thing that gives this bar away is the small red and blue light outside. Once you draw back the heavy curtain and walk into the tiny room adorned with hanging globes and snug leather armchairs you'll want to make it your regular.

Coffy, Winsstr. 65, **T** 0179 211 50 33, www.coffy.de *Tram 1, 2, 3, 4. Daily from 1900. Map 2, F10, p247* Practically pitch black, but presumably going with the Berlin rule that the darker the bar the cooler it must be, Coffy has become quite a favourite among the residents of the surrounding area. The bar has DJs each night after 2200 (the different types of music they play is posted on the website) and there is dancing at the weekends when you have to pay a €3-4 entrance fee.

Fluido, Christburgerstr. 6, **T** 44 04 39 02. *Tram 1. Daily from 2000. Map 2, E10, p247* A deliciously dark, elegant and intimate cocktail bar with a fine selection of drinks. The staff definitely know their stuff, bombarding you with all sorts of different names when you just want a common-or-garden Gin and Tonic. The comfortable leather armchairs and first rate cocktails may make your visit longer than you expected and in the winter it is sometimes necessary to knock on the door to gain entrance. Don't let this daunt you too much. Cocktails €5-10.

Mr. Tibbs, Marienburger Str. 32, **T** 0162 174 72 03. *U-Bahn Senefelder-Platz. Opening hours are anybody's guess. Map 2, E10, p247* This bar, which is a favourite, has a live DJ every night and like most drinking holes in the area is as dark as a winter's night. Monday offers the best Motown soul and funk explosion with 50s' rock 'n' roll chucked in, although it's always pretty empty. The atmosphere is somewhat exclusive but still maintains an air of neighbourhood affability. The music changes daily and the cocktails are cheap and good. Watch out for the raised seating platform and the TV in the girls' toilets.

Weinstein, Lychener Str. 33, **T** 441 18 42, www.weinstein-berlin.de *U-Bahn Eberswalder Str. Mon-Sat 1700-0200, Sun 1800-0200. Map 2, C8, p247* In the midst of the trendy retro bars of Prenzlauerberg this homely, wood-panelled wine bar is a welcome change. The cellar is always fully stocked with wines that slip down delectably. Light snacks such as marinated garlic and olives are available.

Wohnzimmer, Lettestr. 6, **T** 445 54 58. *U-Bahn Eberswalder Str., S-Bahn Prenzlauer Allee. Daily from 1000. Map 2, C9, p247* This café/bar mixes the shabby elegance of its silk-covered divans with the modern, glassy simplicity of its bathrooms and toilet seats. Wohnzimmer has quite a cult following, remaining a favourite with most Humboldt University students for whom it's the perfect place to ponder over Schopenhauer with a cup of peppermint tea late into the night.

Clubs

Icon Club, Cantian Str. 15, **T** 61 28 75 45, www.iconberlin.de *U-Bahn Eberswalder Str. Fri and Sat from 2330. Entrance is about €10. The website give DJ dates, music samples and directions. Map 2, B7, p247* Home to some of the world's finest drum 'n' bass, featuring monthly UK specials, such as DocScott and Grooverider to name a couple. Regular reggae, dance hall, ragga and hiphop nights. An underground venue, with lots of space for dancing and areas to chill out, with two bars and great visuals.

Magnet Club, Greifswalder Str. 212-213, **T** 42 85 13 35, www.magnet-club.de *Tram 2,3,4. Tue from 2100, Fri and Sat from 2300, Sun from 2000. Entrance is €5-15. The website gives each month's programme. Map 2, F10, p247* Magnet tends to attract a friendly, young crowd. During the week it plays host to young local talents such as the indie Karrera Klub but on the weekend it tends to have more pop, dance hall and funk. The club has been known to sneak in the likes of Richard Dorfmeister without informing any of the listings magazines.

Friedrichshain

Bars

Astro-Bar, Simon-Dach-Str. 40, www.astro-bar.de *S-Bahn and U-Bahn Warschauer Str. Daily from 1800. Map 3, C11, p249* You'll think you've wandered into a 70s BBC storage room for *Doctor Who* as you enter and then delve deeper into Astro-Bar. Robots, electric keyboards and old cassette players decorate the walls. The DJs maintain the electro comic feeling and the cocktails flow. A much more interesting alternative to the loungy bars of the district.

Clubs

Casino, Mühlenstr. 26-30, **T** 29 00 97 99, www.casino-bln.com *S-Bahn Ostbahnhof, S-Bahn Warschauer Str. Fri and Sat from 2300. Map 3, D8, p249* Don't be put off by the appearance of this warehouse club. The corrugated iron walls rising up from what looks like a deserted car park are enough to put anyone off but, despite this, Casino still packs them in with live techno and drum 'n' bass acts such as LTJ Bukem, Dr Motte and Paul van Dyk. As well as the main floor there is a lounge upstairs and other chill-out rooms with regular live DJs. Check the website for the programme.

Charlottenburg

Bars

Hefner, Kantstr. 146, **T** 31 01 75 20. *S-Bahn Savignyplatz.
2000-0300. Map 4, D1, p250* This rather pretentious bar on
the corner of Savignyplatz is always littered with beautiful people.
Quite a place to see and be seen. However, the design is simple
and elegant, the service fast and the cocktails slide down very
easily. Lots of fat, leather sofas in which to lounge.

Kumpelnest 3000, Lützowstr. 23, **T** 261 69 18. *U-Bahn
Kurfürstenstr. Sun-Thu 1700-0500, Fri and Sat from 1700. Map 4, E7,
p251* Legendary for not such good reasons – this former brothel
has become quite a meeting place for Berliners. The later it is the
better the dancing gets and the harder of hearing the partially
deaf bar staff become. Always a big hit on the weekends.

Paris Bar, Kantstr. 152, **T** 313 80 52, www.parisbar.de *U-Bahn
Uhlandstr. Daily 1200-0200. Map 4, D2, p250* It was always in the
Paris Bar that the latest art exchanged hands and politicians would
remould and rebuild governments. Nowadays it is pop stars and
celebrities who frequent this classically decorated bar with mirrors
everywhere giving the feeling that it is enormous. The prices are
high but the food is excellent – the blood sausage and potatoes
are generally recommended.

X Bar, Grolmanstr. 51. *S-Bahn Savignyplatz. Daily from 1800.
Map 4, D1, p250* This cocktail bar has an extensive drinks' list
but sadly no beer on tap. The service is excellent and provided
with a smile by dashing barmen.

Kreuzberg

Bars

Haifischbar, Arndtstr. 25, **T** 691 13 52. *U-Bahn Mehringdamm, U-Bahn Gneisenaustr. Sun-Thu 2000-0400, Fri and Sat 2000-0500. Map 3, H1, p248* This bar is often the start of the evening as well as the end of it. The bar staff are friendly and pretty nifty with the cocktails and the room at the back serves sushi. The music is always good, but slightly loungy, and there's always a crowd enjoying themselves.

Roses, Oranienstr. 187, **T** 615 65 70. *U-Bahn Kottbusser Tor, U-Bahn Görlitzer Bahnhof. Daily 2100-0600. Map 3, E4, p248* Roses should be visited just to see the extraordinarily kitsch interior. The bar itself is tiny, the barmen gay as can be, and the walls covered in red, crush velvet with illuminated and flashing Popes and Madonna figures. Predominantly a gay bar but any sexual preference is welcome. An essential stop for any Oranienstrasse bar crawl.

Schnabelbar, Oranienstr. 31, **T** 615 85 34. *U-Bahn Kottbusser Tor. Daily from 2000. Map 3, E4, p248* 'The bar with the Martini Logo' as it is also known is past its prime but it still attracts the punters. The old and decrepit DJ who looks like a cross between a Stones hanger-on and a Hendrix wannabe still manages to spin out some good funk and reggae but the dance floor is pretty cramped.

Würgeengel, Dresdener Str. 122, **T** 615 55 60, www.wuergeengel.de *U-Bahn Kottbusser Tor. Daily from 1900. Map 3, D4, p248* 'Angel of Death' is decorated in plush, red velvet and adorned with 1920s chandeliers. The atmosphere of peccadillo is enticing and usually ensures you stay for much longer than planned. The prices are high (€5-8.50) and the cocktails deadly.

Clubs

SO36, Oranienstr. 190, **T** 61 40 13 06, www.so36.de *U-Bahn Kottbusser Tor, U-Bahn Görlitzer Bahnhof. Mon from 2300, Wed and Fri from 2200, Sat from 2100, Sun from 1900. Map 3, F6, p248*
The name of this club is the postcode of Kreuzberg and has always been a favourite with residents. Enjoying cult status among the gay scene, SO36 also caters to the average party crowd. It often has live events, hosting only recently the Skatalites, but also has regular club nights. On Sundays the club hosts Café Fatal's boogie, swing and salsa dance classes and the Electric Ballroom group always plays on Mondays. See the website for the specifics.

Schöneberg

Bars

Bar am Lützowplatz, Lützowplatz 7, **T** 262 68 07, www.baramluetzowplatz.com *U-Bahn Nollendorfplatz. Daily 1400-0400. Map 4, D6, p250* One cocktail here is enough to send you right off the deep end. Bar am Lützowplatz is known for its 17-m long bar and highly alcoholic cocktails, which are matched by rather high prices. A place for the rich and beautiful to meet. During happy hour, (1400-2100), the cocktails are half price.

Billy Wilder's, Potsdamer Str. 2, **T** 26 55 48 61. *S-Bahn and U-Bahn Potsdamer Platz. Daily 0900-0200. Map 6, C3, p253*
Situated at the edge of the futuristic Sony Center and as part of the Arsenal/Film Museum complex, Billy Wilder's has all the trappings of a film bar. Decorated with pictures of Wilder's classics such as *Some Like It Hot*, this hot and steamy bar is fairly pricey, but convenient on winter nights after a trip to the movies.

Mutter, Hohenstaufenstr. 4, **T** 216 49 90. *U-Bahn Nollendorfplatz. Daily 1000-0400. Map 4, G6, p250* Despite looking very parochial on the outside, Mutter has a lot of style once you walk through the door. The bar is small but apart from this there is plenty of room and a trip down the corrugated iron corridor to the toilets is somewhat out of the ordinary. Sushi and Thai food are served from 1800 and an extensive list of wines, beers and cocktails is available.

Clubs

90 Grad, Dennewitzstr. 37, **T** 23 00 59 54, www.90grad.de *U-Bahn Kurfürstenstr., U-Bahn Bülowstr. Wed 2100-0300, Fri and Sat from 2300. Map 4, F9, p251* Formerly a club that attracted the cream of the house and techno DJs, as well as a pretty mixed crowd in sexual persuasion and social position, 90 Grad has changed pretty dramatically. The place to be, with a strict door policy and beautiful people everywhere especially behind the bar. The club itself is divided into three exotic-looking rooms and nights are always debauched…just as long as you bring lots of cash.

Neukölln

Bars

Ankerklause, Kottbusser Brücke corner of Maybauchufer, **T** 693 56 49, www.ankerklause.de *U-Bahn Schönleinstr., U-Bahn Kottbuser Tor. Tue-Sun 1000-0400, Mon 1600-0400. Map 3, G5, p248* This 'anchor den' overlooking the Landwehrkanal is a slightly more Captain Pugwash than Captain Haddock but remains a chilled-out favourite. A funky, fishy design pervades throughout and the sandwich melts are reputedly the best in town. Note the jukebox with a complete catalogue of rock 'n' roll.

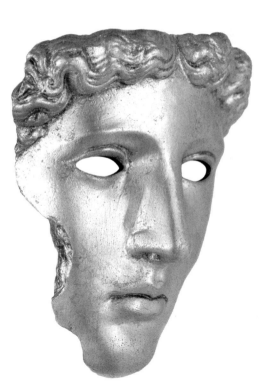

Berlin has always been a fantastic city to soak up cutting-edge theatre, innovative dance and stunningly good music from jazz to opera to folk. The arts scene has had a reputation for being vibrant and incredibly important to Berliners as well as politicians who continue to put money into it even when the city is floundering under so many debts.

The classical music scene is world-renowned and the presence of foreign conductors and artists such as Sir Simon Rattle and Daniel Barenboim in its most high-profile institutions has given the Berlin arts scene even more international acclaim.

Berlin has always been home to talented playwrights and plays performed in various theatres are guaranteed to be inventive and entertaining.

The jazz scene is large and ranges from the JazzFest (p190) to small gigs or jamming sessions, all of which normally stick to the more traditional sides of things. This is also a city which attracts top names in pop and rock so all the big tours such as U2, Kylie and Supertramp will always stop here.

Berlin has always been associated with cinema and today is no different with Wim Wenders and Werner Herzog still driving film to the cutting edge. There are posters for events everywhere, especially along the Kurfürstendamm and Unter den Linden. Otherwise watch out for the English listings magazine the *Ex-Berliner* which is free and can be found in most cafés.

Cinema

Germany has had a historic role in world cinema. Berlin has been at the forefront of cinema even from the days before it supposedly existed. When the Lumière brothers demonstrated cinematography with their *L'Arrivée d'un Train* in Paris in 1895 it had already been demonstrated by Max Skladanowsky's *Bioscope* in Berlin two months earlier! However, Berlin soon became renowned as the centre of Germany's fledgling film industry, and by 1905 there were 16 movie theatres in the city. Austrian and German actors, cinematographers and directors were pioneers in the new film art. Hollywood would not be what it is today without the impact of the likes of Rainer Werner Fassbinder, Fritz Lang, Friedrich Murnau, Wolfgang Petersen, Billy Wilder, Wim Wenders and others.

Between 1920 and 1932, the so-called "Golden Age" of early German cinema, before the Nazis ruined its reputation, cinema from Berlin led the way for future filmmakers. Beginning with the great pioneering silent films of the 1920s, such as *Metropolis*, *Nosferatu*, and *Das Cabinet des Dr. Caligari*, and continuing with the advent of sound after 1929 – *Der blaue Engel* and *M* – German film became synonymous with distinctive technique and style. The sound techniques, lighting and set design of German expressionistic films such as *Caligari* and *Metropolis* were the precursors of the Hollywood film noir. In the 1920s and 1930s, directors like Billy Wilder (*Some Like It Hot*), and others left Europe for Hollywood. Even today the bigger budgets and greater exposure of the US tempt Berlin directors such as Roland Emmerich (*Independence Day, Godzilla*) and Wolfgang Petersen (*Outbreak, In the Line of Fire, Das Boot*).

There was a big content crisis in German film in the 90s with an overwhelming and gruelling amount of relationship comedies. However, this seems to be over and young filmmakers experimenting with digital video and authentic stories from Germany (and not from Hollywood) like Andreas Dresen, Rudolf Thomes and Thomas Arslan for example, with his Berlin trilogy, are already renowned in Germany. Last year *Der Schuh des Manitu* by Michael Herbig was a tremendous success and was seen by more than nine million people. It was a comedy about the German cowboy-and-Indian-films in the 70s. The topic isn't very original, but at least the film is.

Today Berlin has over 250 screens in over 90 cinemas. They are scattered right across the city, ranging from multi-complexes, such as the various cinemas at the Sony Center to independent *Kinos* hidden down the back streets of Kreuzberg, Prenzlauerberg and the like, where you can sip on a bottle of Becks whilst watching the latest underground film or a Fellini classic. Listed are some of the best *Kinos* in town, but first you'll need to be familiar with the *Kino* lingo: *Kino* – cinema; *Kinotag* – cinema day, when tickets are half price, usually Mondays, Tuesdays or Wednesdays; *OF* – *Originalfassung* (original version); *OmU* – *Original mit Untertiteln* (original with subtitles). The best place to find film showing times and locations is in the *Kino* section of *Zitty* and *Tip*, the listings magazines. For listings in English there is the free magazine the *Ex-Berliner*.

During the summer months the various *Freiluftkinos* (open-air cinemas) are very popular. These are situated in Volkspark Friedrichshain, Potsdamer Platz, the Museumsinsel and Kreuzberg. Check the listings for programmes, and remember to bring a jumper.

Babylon, Dresdner Str. 126, **T** 61 60 96 93. *U-Bahn Kottbusser Tor. Map 3, D4, p248* Screening predominantly *OmU*, this independent *Kino* just off Kottbusser Tor, is perfect for catching up with the latest releases.

Blow-Up, Immanuelkirchstr. 14, **T** 442 86 62. *Tram 2,3,4. Map 2, F10, p247* The essential in independent cinemas – two small cinemas screening the most recent in alternative cinema and some must-see classics, chiefly in *OF* and *OmU*. Ideal to go out in the evening and then sample some of Prenzlauerberg's finest bars, such as *Coffy* (p166), *Mr. Tibbs* (p166) and for that perfect cocktail *Fluido* (p166).

CinemaxX, Potsdamerstr. 5, Potsdamer Platz, **T** 44 31 63 16, www.cinemaxx.de *S-Bahn and U-Bahn Potsdamer Platz. Map 6, C3, p253* This is the place to go to see films in English. It is the biggest complex Berlin has to offer with three screens regularly showing films in English. Only Hollywood mainstream is shown here.

CineStar Sony Center, Potsdamerstr. 4, **T** 26 06 64 00, www.cinestar.de *S-Bahn and U-Bahn Potsdamer Platz. Map 6, B4, p253* Another big complex showing purely Hollywood mainstream. Films in English are shown every day and Tuesday is *Kino Tag*. There are eight screens and because you only have to show a ticket to get into the general area it is possible to see movie after movie.

Hackescher Höfe, Rosenthalerstr. 40/41, **T** 283 46 03, www.hackesche-hoefe.org *S-Bahn Hackescher Markt. Map 7, B9, p255* Just opposite the Hackescher Markt S-Bahn exit this independent cinema offers a fantastic range of current and classic films, often in *OF* or *OmU*. The repertoire is normally foreign and arthouse. Berlin classics, such as *Berlin Babylon* and Wim Wenders' *Der Himmel über Berlin* are shown several times daily, perfect for a rainy day and a bit of Berlin history.

International Kino, Karl-Marx-Allee 33, **T** 24 75 60 11. *U-Bahn Schillingstr. Map 2, H9, p247* For the ultimate *Kino* experience in Berlin. Do not be deceived by the aggressive, concrete exterior, for the inside takes you back to 1963, when the *Kino* was built. Retro, plush red carpets, chandeliers and a fantastic mirrored bar all add to the atmosphere of this GDR relic. International films are shown. Most are dubbed into German but if you're not at one with the language simply go for the unique atmosphere.

Dance

The dance scene in Berlin is becoming increasingly large as the interest in contemporary dance greatens and the numbers of dancers coming to Berlin multiplies. The dance scene's profile has become even higher recently since the mayor of Berlin, Klaus Wowereit, mentioned its importance so often in his election speeches. With choreographers from New York and Hong Kong, contemporary dance has looked ever further afield and it is now common to see touring companies from the capital in any major dance festival in the world.

Berlin has always had a strong classical dance tradition and even here there is room for innovative and cutting-edge productions such as *Der Traum des Minotaurs* (The Minotaur's Dream) at the Komische Oper. However, if a conventional but brilliantly fine-tuned production of Tchaikovsky is more your scene, the city will not disappoint.

Deutsche Oper, Bismarckstr. 35, **T** 343 84 01, www.deutsche-oper.berlin.de *U-Bahn Deutsche Oper. Map 5, F5, p252* The Deutsche Oper (see also p185) is much smaller than the Staatsoper (see p184) with a ballet corps of only 30. The director is Sylviane Baynard who has gently nudged the ballet's style towards a more forward-looking position.

Hebbel-Theater, Stresemannstr. 13A, **T** 25 90 04 27, www.hebbel-theater.de *S-Bahn and U-Bahn Friedrichstr. Map 4, F12, p251* Home of the avant-garde, this theatre has propelled modern dance into Berlin through hosting companies such as Mikhail Barishnikov's White Oak Dance Project. Each February the theatre puts on *Tanz im Winter*, a three-week dance festival; and each summer *Tanz im August*, also for three weeks.

Komische Oper, Behrenstr. 55-7, **T** 20 26 00, www.komische-oper-berlin.de *S-Bahn Unter den Linden, U-Bahn Französische Str. Map 7, F4, p254* The Komische Oper (see also p185) has Spain's Blance Li as its ballet director. On the classically elegant stage hidden behind a drab exterior there are plenty of experimental ballets regularly performed.

Staatsoper Unter den Linden, Unter den Linden 5-7, **T** 20 35 40, www.staatsoper-berlin.org *U-Bahn Französische Str. Map 7, F7, p255* The Staatsoper (see also p184) with 64 members is the largest of Berlin's ballets. Vladimir Malakhov became director of the ballet in 2002 and will only add to its already impressive reputation as the home of romantic tradition with productions such as *Giselle* and *Dornröschen* (Sleeping Beauty) performed regularly.

Theater am Halleschen Ufer, Hallesches Ufer 32, **T** 251 06 55, www.thub.de *U-Bahn Hallesches Tor, U-Bahn Möckernbrücke.* This theatre supports contemporary, independent dance groups and has been actively involved in the success of some of the city's young talent. If you are very interested in contemporary dance try and go to a matinee production as there are usually audience discussions afterwards. The Solo Duo festival held here in March reflects global dance trends.

Music

Rock and Pop

Berlin attracts all the top international pop and rock acts. Recently the various concerts and stadiums have played host to the likes of Destiny's Child, Wyclef Jean, Kid Loco, Supertramp and Roger Waters. The venues in Berlin tend to be smaller than in London, which makes for a more intimate gig-like atmosphere. There are posters everywhere around Berlin advertising the latest offerings but the best way to find out what is going on is to check the listings. See p217.

Arena, Eichenstr. 4, **T** 533 73 33, www.arena-berlin.de *S-Bahn Treptower Park. Map 3, G11, p249* A former bus depot that can hold over 7,000 people and attracting artists such as Prodigy and Chemical Brothers.

ColumbiaFritz, Columbiadamm 13-21, **T** 698 09 80, www.columbiafritz.de *U-Bahn Platz der Luftbrücke.* A smaller version of next door's Columbiahalle, this former US Forces cinema has recently played host to the likes of Gomez and Wyclef Jean. The artists tend to jump all over the place so don't worry if you're stuck at the back.

Columbiahalle, Columbiadamm 13-21, **T** 698 09 80, www.columbiahalle.de *U-Bahn Platz der Luftbrücke.* With a capacity for 3,500 people the Columbiahalle is more popular with bands such as Status Quo, Nick Cave, Manic Street Preachers and Berlin's own Element of Crime.

Neues Tempodrom, Möckernstr. 10, **T** 69 53 38 85, www.tempodrom.de *S-Bahn Anhalter Bahnhof. Map 4, E11, p251* Having moved from its location in Potsdamer Platz to Ostbahnhof and finally to Anhalter Bahnhof, the Tempodrom has a slightly smaller capacity than Columbiahalle, but there is also a small area for 500 people next to it – the Liquidrom, an aquatic concert hall (www.liquidrom.com) where the likes of Vanessa Mae and Melissa Etheridge have performed.

Waldbühne, Glockenturmstr./Passenheimerstr., **T** 0180 53 32 433. *U-Bahn Olympia-Stadion (Ost), S-Bahn Pichelsberg.* An open-air venue in Charlottenburg that can hold up to 22,000 people. Recent acts have included Supertramp and Depeche Mode.

World Music

Berlin provides an audience as well as many a venue for World Music. Fans will find that jazz fusion meets Afro Caribbean beats and Latin dance combines with Indonesian instrumental folk rock. There are many venues catering to all sorts of communities from Poland, Turkey, Russia, Brazil, Ireland and North Africa. *Zitty*, *Tip* and the *Ex-Berliner* will give information (see p217) about events, but also tune into SFB4 MultiKulti radio on 106.8 FM.

Hackesches Hof Theater, Rosenthalerstr. 40-41, **T** 28 73 25 87. *S-Bahn Hackescher Markt. Map 7, B9, p255* If you walk through to the second courtyard of the Hackescher Höfe complex you can't miss the signs advertising Yiddish concerts. The venue, which is small, is situated near the New Synagogue. It offers daily concerts of Yiddish and East European folk music.

Haus der Kulturen der Welt, John-Foster-Dulles Allee 10, **T** 39 78 71 75, www.hkw.de *S-Bahn Bellevue, Bus 100. Map 4, A8, p251* The House of World Cultures, located in the Tiergarten, is a leading centre for contemporary arts and a venue for projects designed to break artistic boundaries. It is Berlin's largest World Music venue. Fine arts, theatre, music, literature and film are shown and heard here, making it one of the city's most interesting cultural centres.

Werkstatt der Kulturen, Wissmannstr. 31-42, **T** 622 20 24, www.werkstatt-der-kulturen.de *U-Bahn Hermannplatz.* This small space is used very well in promoting the diverse nature of the city. Art, theatre, fashion and music from Spain, India and the Ukraine and other countries exist here, creating a very special atmosphere.

Jazz

There is a fully formed and growing jazz scene in Berlin with around 40 venues throughout the city. The music tends to be more traditional jazz rather than anything else, but there are jam sessions and young contemporary talent to be found around town too. Jazz has its own radio station in the city – JazzRadio (101.9 Fm), which also has a website in both English and German (www. Jazzradio.net). If visiting in the autumn try and make it to the Berlin JazzFest (see p190).

B-Flat, Rosenthalestr. 13, **T** 280 63 49. *U-Bahn Weinmeisterstr. Daily from 2100. Map 7, A9, p255* Previously a *Geheimtip* (secret tip) for jazz fans and musicians, B-Flat has now turned more mainstream but you can still find the odd post-Headhunters Herbie Hancock aspirants. The club also hosts tango and salsa nights.

Bebop Bar, Willibald-Alexis-Str. 40, **T** 694 11 01, www.bebop-bar.de *U-Bahn Mehringdamm. Concerts from 2200 Tue, Fri-Sun. Map 3, H1, p248* More of a jazz pub than a jazz club, Bebop Bar offers live music five days a week. The restrained lighting makes for a warm and welcoming atmosphere. Along with jazz, folk music nights are often hosted.

Junction Bar, Gneisenaustr. 18, **T** 694 66 02, www.junction-bar.de *U-Bahn Gneisenaustr. Daily 1100-0500. Concerts normally around 2200. Map 3, H1, p248* This jazz club located in a cellar on the busy Gneisenaustrasse hosts nightly concerts, whether it be jazz, blues, funk or even rap – as long as there's a jazzy feel. There is always dancing after concerts with music provided by DJs. The bar can get very packed so make sure you get there early.

Quasimodo, Kantstr. 12a, **T** 312 80 86, www.quasimodo.de *S-Bahn and U-Bahn Zoologischer Garten. Concerts daily from 2200. Map 4, D2, p250* A legendary jazz bar that has played host to many world-famous artists including Prince. A good student night is Wednesday when there are jam sessions and the entrance is less expensive and includes a drink at the bar.

Classical

A visitor could stay in Berlin for a year and still not experience all the city has to offer in terms of classical music. With seven orchestras, three opera houses and a plethora of independent companies the city is indeed well endowed. This is a result of the legacy of communism and unlimited state support for the arts, as well as German musical tradition. The existence of two Berlins also contributed to the number of music companies. The state support for the arts remains very strong and was seen most recently in the signing-up of conductor Sir Simon Rattle to the Berlin Philharmonie at a time when the city was verging on bankruptcy. There are constant spats with the government over funding, but when the likes of conductor Daniel Barenboim put their foot down the money seems to come. It's debatable how long the nearly bankrupt city can maintain such provision but many argue it is necessary for Berlin's economy. The city is also home to many music academies that draw some of the world's best young music talent. These institutions regularly host recitals by soloists as well as providing a venue for other musicians.

Concert Halls

Philharmonie, Herbert-von-Karajan-Str. 1, **T** 25 48 81 32, www.berlin-philharmonic.com *S-Bahn and U-Bahn Potsdamer Platz. Map 6, B3, p253* The Berlin Philharmonic Orchestra is one of the world's most celebrated, and the concert hall is one of the world's most bold and successful attempts at acoustic modernism. Sir Simon Rattle became conductor of the orchestra in 2002.

Universität der Künste, Hardenbergstr. 33, **T** 31 85 23 74. *S-Bahn and U-Bahn Zoologischer Garten, U Ernst-Reuter-Platz. Map 4, D2, p250* Previously the Hochschule der Künste, this institution recently took the name "university" in a bid to become better known. The building is a 70s' cement block but functions very well acoustically. Here you will find young soloists, orchestras and even the likes of the Pasadena Roof Orchestra.

Kammermusiksaal, Herbert-von-Karajan-Str. 1, **T**25 48 81 32. *S-Bahn and U-Bahn Potsdamer Platz. Map 6, B3, p253* Part of the Berlin Philharmonie, and housed within the same building, this smaller hall has all the acoustic accoutrements of its bigger brother. The stalls provide amazing listening, but if you sit behind the orchestra (where the seats are much cheaper), it's a different story.

Opera

Staatsoper, Unter den Linden 7, **T** 20 35 45 55, www.staatsoper-berlin.org *U-Bahn Französische Str. Map 7, F7, p255* The leadership of this exquisitely restored opera house is under Daniel Barenboim. With traditional operas and ballets on offer this is one of Berlin's most popular classical venues. Unsold tickets are available for €10 before a performance.

Komische Oper, Behrenstr. 55-57, **T** 47 99 74 00, www.komische-oper-berlin.de *S-Bahn Unter den Linden. Map 7, F4, p254* Don't be put off by the drab, bleak building of the Komische Oper, inside is one of the most well-hidden, charming secrets of the city. The plush opera house puts on more alternative productions than the Staatsoper, which are lighter in theme and very innovative.

Deutsche Oper, Bismarckstr. 34-37, **T** 343 84 01, www.deutsche-oper.berlin.de *U-Bahn Deutsche Oper. Map 5, F5, p252* The only one of Berlin's opera companies to be housed in a modern building, the Deutsche Oper offers a wide range with some recent 20th-century masterpieces such as Bartók. The new intendant Udo Zimmerman has mentioned he wants to introduce some contemporary works.

Theatre

Berlin remains a major cultural centre with dramatic arts playing a dominant role. The city has a rich theatrical history. Bertolt Brecht, after leaving Hollywood in the 1940s due to the rise of McCarthyism, settled in East Berlin and founded the famous Berliner Ensemble with his wife Helene Weigel. Although a card-carrying communist who toed the DDR line, Brecht still managed to maintain his Swiss bank account until he died. The actor and director Max Reinhardt (1873-1943), who was also a great theatre reformer, worked in Berlin at the Deutsches Theater. As well as setting up the Kammerspiele he also produced plays for the Berliner Ensemble. Today there is a host of theatres that offer dynamic, vibrant and extremely well-produced plays from more traditional performances to modern plays and monologues.The Volksbühne or "People's Stage" attracts bohos and conservatives alike. More experimental alternative theatre is on show here.

Berliner Ensemble, Bertolt-Brecht-Platz 1, **T** 282 31 60, www.berliner-ensemble.de *S-Bahn and U-Bahn Friedrichstr.* *Map 7, C4, p254* The Berliner Ensemble, founded by Bertolt Brecht and Helene Weigel in 1949 after the ground-breaking production of *Mouther Courage,* moved to the lavish neo-baroque Theater am Schiffbauerdamm in 1954. Its productions are still innovative and avant-garde.

Deutsches Theater/Kammerspiele des Deutschen Theaters, Schumannstr. 13A, **T** 28 44 12 25, www.deutsches-theater.berlin.net *S-Bahn and U-Bahn Friedrichstr. Map 7, B3, p254* This elegant 19th-century theatre houses the resident state drama company. The productions are always undoubtedly good with a wide repertoire from German classics such as Lessing's *Emilia Galotti* to modern experiments like *Doktor Caligari*. Contemporary foreign playwrights such as Neil La Bute are also popular.

Maxim Gorki Theater, Am Festungsgraben 2, **T** 20 22 11 15, www.gorki.de *S-Bahn and U-Bahn Friedrichstr. Map 7, E7, p255* The Gorki Theater looks rather grand from the outside but once inside it seems almost like a doll's-house stage. However, this by no means diminishes its productions. The plays are usually slick, funny and poignant. Chekhov is a favourite here but young German playwrights are also represented.

Volksbühne, Rosa-Luxemburg-Platz, **T** 247 67 72/76 94, www.volksbuehne-berlin.de *U-Bahn Rosa-Luxemburg-Platz. Map 7, A11, p255* A predominantly political theatre following the tradition set by its name "The People's Stage". The two directors, Sebastian Hartmann and Thomas Bischoff, contribute to the success of the playhouse with plays attracting audiences from all parts of the community.

Arts and entertainment

In Berlin you will find a festival to celebrate everything. From the Berlin International Film Festival, which is the largest in the world, second only to Cannes, to the St Christopher Street Day Parade, a gay pride parade commemorating the New York Stonewall riots.

There are plenty of musical festivals, such as the Fete de la Music and the Berlin JazzFest. And, of course, nobody can ignore the outrageous Love Parade. More political alternatives are the Fuck Parade and there is also scope for more young, up and coming festivals like the Karneval der Kulturen.

The festivals are dispersed throughout the year and it is a good idea to try and come for one of them as they all show Berlin in an even more accommodating and friendly light, not to mention the fact they bring in an exciting and international crowd.

February

Berlin International Film Festival (2 weeks in mid-February) The festival, with over 300 films, is spread over a week and a half and is divided into different categories to be judged. Short documentaries are shown after large studio productions at various cinemas around the city. This gives it an arty yet accessible feel. The main hub of the festival is around Potsdamer Platz giving this otherwise bleak, atmosphereless futuristic centre a glitzy and glamorous feel. More information from www.berlinale.de

April

Sehnsüchte (six days at the end of April/beginning of May) This international student film festival in Potsdam is one of the greatest of its kind in Europe. Students of the Academy for Film and Television Potsdam-Babelsberg (www.hff-potsdam.de) present over 150 films from students and amateur filmmakers. The festival takes place in the Thalia Arthouse Cinemas in Potsdam-Babelsberg.

May

Karneval der Kulturen (four days in May/June) This colourful carnival and parade in Kreuzberg celebrates Berlin's ethnic diversity. There is a fun vibe with stalls and stages on the Saturday and a bright parade on the Sunday. For more information: www.karneval-berlin.de

June

Christopher Street Day Parade (mid-to late June) The most flamboyant festival in Berlin. This gay and lesbian parade is always very loud and outrageous. Not for the faint-hearted. The parade starts on the Kurfürstendamm and ends at the Victory Angel in Tiergarten. For more information: www.csd-berlin.de

Fête de la Musique (21 June) This free day of music takes place in various venues around Berlin (www.lafetedelamusique.de). The music performed ranges from rock to electric pop to reggae, ragga, polka, jazz, world music and folk. The atmosphere is up lifting and this street event should not, and logistically cannot, be missed.

July

Love Parade (2nd Saturday in July) The original love parade (www.loveparade.de) in Tiergarten attracts millions of visitors every year. Since 2001 when the Love Parade was denied the label of a political event, it has been up to the organizers to clean up the city in the parade's wake. As the costs are very high, this is another factor endangering its future.

Fuck Parade (2nd Saturday in July) The Fuck Parade in Mitte is known as a more "political" alternative than the Love Parade. Since the government tried to put an end to the parade it has advertised itself as a "demonstration for a right to demonstrate". For more information: **T** (069) 94 35 90 90, www.fuckparade.de

---

October

JazzFest Berlin (four days late October/early November) The JazzFest (www.berlinerfestspiele.de) is one of the most important festivals of contemporary jazz with an array of international artists. The entertainment takes place in various venues in and around Berlin such as Haus der Berliner Festspiele and Quasimodo (p183).

Berlin offers all the different types of shopping you could ask for, from swanky, chic stores like KaDeWe to second-hand holes where you pay by the weight of your clothes. You will also find young designer jewellers, antiquated map and bookshops, delicious food emporiums and tourist shops that seem to be 100 years out of date. The music shops range from the enormous, having everything you've ever wanted or everything that you haven't been able to find anywhere else, to tiny and specialist, which despite their size will keep you amused for hours.

Second-hand shops proliferate in the back streets selling everything from 70s' green leather Adidas-designed motorcycle police trousers to 20s' ball gowns. Retro furniture shops are all the rage and if markets are what floats your boat then you're in luck. Every Saturday there are at least four of them. Shops open 0900-1000 in the week, closing as late as 1900-2000. On a Saturday they open 0900-1000 but shut at 1600.

Department Stores

Galeries Lafayette, Französische Str. 23, **T** 20 94 80. *U-Bahn Stadtmitte, S-Bahn and U-Bahn Friedrichstr. Mon-Fri 0930-2000, Sat 0900-1600. Map 7, G5, p254* A highly elegant department store without being too exclusive. The airy, glass design of the building from the architect Jean Nouvel makes shopping here a quite pleasant experience. The food hall is well worth a visit.

KaDeWe, Tauentzienstr. 21-4, **T** 21210. *U -Bahn Wittenbergplatz. Mon-Fri 0930-2000, Sat 0900-1600. Map 4, E4, p250* The Kaufhaus des Westens (department store of the West) is the biggest on the continent. It is akin to Harrods but so much more elegant. The sixth-floor food hall with its gourmet bar and delicatessen is impressive and likely to tempt seafood lovers. Exhibitions, fashion shows and book signings are a regular feature. See also p81.

Kaufhof, Alexanderplatz 9, **T** 24 74 32 65. *S-Bahn and U-Bahn Alexanderplatz. Mon-Fri 0900-2000, Sat 0900-1600. Map 7, C12, p255* This 70s building, which has now become quite a Berlin icon with photographs of it appearing in bars throughout town, is a standard department store with the elegance or luxury of KaDeWe.

Naturkaufhaus, Schlossstr. 101, **T** 79 73 716. *U-Bahn Schlossstr. Mon-Fri 1000-2000, Sat 1000-1600.* Berlin's first environmentally friendly department store is located in this main shopping street of Steglitz. The goods range from organic food to organic clothes, cosmetics and wine.

Quartier 206, Friedrichstr. 71, **T** 20 94 68 00. *U-Bahn Stadtmitte. Mon-Fri 1000-2000, Sat 1000-1600. Map 7, F5, p254* The height of designer fashion exists on Mitte's Friedrichstrasse. Gucci, Kenzo and Manolo Blahnik can be found behind the chic black marble exterior.

Wertheim, Kurfürstendamm 231, **T** 88 03 00. *U-Bahn Kurfürsten-damm. Mon-Fri 0930-2000, Sat 0900-1600. Map 4, E1, p250* The various Wertheims are known for their delectable foodstuffs. A fantastic place to purchase Christmas necessities especially delicious German chocolate and *Lebkuchen* (speciality German biscuits).

Fashion

Hallhuber, Kurfürstendamm. 13, Gloriapassage, **T** 88 12 078. *U-Bahn Kurfürstendamm. Mon-Fri 1000-2000, Sat 1000-1600. Map 4, E3, p250* German high street fashion which, contrary to popular belief, is actually very trendy. The clothes, for both men and women, are à la mode, well cut and inexpensive.

Stephanie Schenk, Gipsstr. 9, **T** 28 39 07 85. *S-Bahn Hackescher Markt, U-Bahn Weinmeisterstr. Map 7, A8, p255* A local Berlin designer whose exquisite clothes are expensive but beautiful.

Double Happiness, Krausnickstr. 6, **T** 28 09 77 41. *S-Bahn Hackescher Markt. Mon-Fri 1200-1900, Sat 1100-1800. Map 7, B7, p255* A delightful little Japanese and Chinese shop in the back streets behind Oranienburgerstrasse. Clothes, such as silk kimonos, are on sale at rather inexpensive prices. You can also buy bowls and chopsticks and fountains for your garden. A wonderful place to visit as it is so relaxing and the lady who owns it so friendly.

Tosh, Sredzkistr. 56, **T** 44 03 83 50. *Tram 1, but close to U-Bahn Senefelderplatz or U-Bahn Eberswalder Str. Mon-Fri 1100-1900, Sat 1100-1500. Map 2, D9, p247* A small, private jewellers with the workshop on the premises. There are stunning designs, vibrant colours, friendly staff and the not too expensive price tags. Strongly recommended but be prepared to be tempted by everything.

Markets

Strasse des 17. Juni, Strasse des 17. Juni, **T** 26 55 00 96. *U-Bahn Ernst-Reuter-Platz, S-Bahn Tiergarten. Weekends 1000-1700. Map 4, B3, p250* This rather over-priced market sells early 20th-century *objets d'art* as well as a good selection of clothes, books and records. An enjoyable way to spend a Sunday morning.

Treptower Hallentrödel, Eichenstr. 4. *S-Bahn Treptower Park. 1000-1700. Map 3, G11, p249* This is a real flea market where locals go to buy vacuums, lightbulbs, pens, records, clothes, televisions, beds and anything else. It is not fashionable at all but a lot of fun. Do not take pictures as the vendors are likely to get angry.Lenné, Peter Joseph 53

Music and Books

Der Kleine Buchladen, Weydingerstr. 14-16, **T** 2472-4683, www.kleinerbuchladen.de *U-Bahn Rosa Luxemburg Platz. Map 7, A12, p255* It is the PDS bookshop and also has a lot of second-hand material from GDR days. Those interested in political history will find it a gold mine.

D-Fens, Greifswalder Str. 224, T 44 34 22 50. *Tram 2, 3, 4. Mon-Fri 1200-1900, Sat 1200-1500. Map 2, F10, p247* Home to Berlin independent and house record labels, the owner of this tiny converted garage is a DJ himself and happy to help with any enquiries.

Dussmann Das Kulturkaufhaus, Friedrichstr. 90, **T** 20 250. *S-Bahn and U-Bahn Friedrichstr. Mon-Sat 1000-2200. Map 7, E5, p254* An extraordinarily wide range of music is on sale. All floors house German books On the top floor there is an English and French selection. Internet portals are on the top floor but are expensive and next to them is a lounge area underneath a glass atrium.

Hugendubel, Tauentzienstr. 13, **T** 21 40 60. *U-Bahn Wittenberg-platz. Mon-Fri 0930-2000, Sat 1000-1600. Map 4, E4, p250*
Hugendubel's enormous section of books is housed over four floors. There is a very large English language selection. Another branch is at Friedrichstrasse 83, **T** 20 63 51 00.

World of Music (WOM), Augsburger Str. 36-42, **T** 88 57 240. *U-Bahn Augsburger Str. Mon-Fri 1000-2000, Sat 0900-1600. Map 4, E3, p250* A straightforward CD emporium with branches around Berlin.

Second-hand clothes and knick-knacks

Bits and Pieces, Lemanns Colonialwaren Grolmannstr. 46, **T** 883 3942. *S-Bahn Savigny Platz. Tue-Fri 1400-1830. Map 4, D1, p250* Noted for its leather suitcases, ships in bottles, globes, embroidered handkerchiefs and anything else of this ilk. A shop that revels in being 100 years out of date.

Garage, Ahornstr. 2, **T** 21 12 760. *U-Bahn Nollendorfplatz. Mon-Wed 1100-1900, Thu, Fri 1100-2000, Sat 1000-1600. Map 4, E6, p250* Very cheap second-hand shop where prices are per kilo.

Humana, Karl-Liebknecht-Str. 30, **T** 24 23 000. *S-Bahn and U-Bahn Alexanderplatz. Mon-Wed 1000-1930, Thu, Fri 1100-2000, Sat 1000-1600. Map 7, B12, p255* An enormous charity, second-hand department store.

Schönauser, Neue Schönauserstr. 18, **T** 31 26 523. *S-Bahn Hackescher Markt, U-Bahn Weinmeisterstr. Mon-Fri 1200-2000, Sat 1100-1600. Map 7, B10, p255* A fantastic shop in which you can spend lots of money buying totally useless but wonderful things like flashing fish lights, retro ice packs, 70s' bags, chairs and furniture in general. Definitely worth a visit.

Berlin's sporting prowess has come under fire recently due to a decline in football victories from their homegrown team, Hertha BSC, a risein drugs scandals, and the bankruptcy of Leo Kirch, causing a debacle equivalent to that of ITV Digital.

However, in Berlin you will have access to every sport you can think of, from watching football to playing it, to ice-skating, kickboxing and to the more relaxing Turkish baths. Most swimming pools and other sports facilities are open to anybody, but some require you to be a member of an organized association or *Verband*, which makes things quite difficult.

Berlin will host the FIFA World Cup in 2006.

Canoeing

Kanu Connection, Köpenickerstr. 9, **T** 61 22 686. *Mon-Fri 1000-1900, Sat 0900-1300. €20-27 per day. U-Bahn Schlesisches Tor. Map 3, C6, p248* A most recommendable way to see the city. From here you can explore Kreuzberg's canals or the forests to the east.

Ice-Skating

Eisstadion Berlin Wilmersdorf, Fritz-Wildung-Str. 9, **T** 82 41 012. *Oct-mid Mar, Mon, Wed, Fri 0900-1730, 1930-2200, Tue, Thu 0900-1730, Sat 0900-2200, Sun 1000-1800. €3, €1.50 concessions per two hours; ice skates available to rent inside. S-Bahn Hohenzollerndamm.* Outdoor ice stadium with an outer and inner rink for both figure and speed skating.

spas

Thermen am Europa-Center, Nürnbergerstr. 7, **T** 25 75 760, www.thermen-berlin.de *Mon-Sat 1000 -2400, Sun 1000-2100. €9.20 first hour, €4.10 thereafter, €17.90 day card. Family card (3 hrs, 1 adult, 1 child, Mon-Wed 1000-1600) €14.30. S-Bahn and U-Bahn Zoolögischer Garten, U-Bahn Kürfurstendamm. Map 4, E4, p250* Thermen is described as an oasis of calm undisturbed by the noise, stress and chaos of the city and for once advertising is telling the truth. This spa has saunas, aqua gymnastics and swimming pools with water with salts from the North Sea and Dead Sea rather than chlorine. There is also a separate 'Wellness' spa facility which provides massages, facials, manicures, flotariums, and something entitled Cleopatra's bath! However, these all cost quite a lot more. A fantastic getaway in the middle of the city.

blub Badeparadies, Buschkrugallee. 64, **T** 60 90 60, www.blubberlin.de *Daily 1000-2300. Prices for adults at the weekend. 1 ½ hrs €9.20, 4 hrs €10.70, day card €13.30, Family card (Thu only, except holidays, for 4 hrs) adult €7.10, from 13 years and student €6.10, 2-12 years old €5. Weekdays and children's tickets are cheaper. U-Bahn Grenzallee.* These enormous baths are outside the centre of town but worth the trek. The emphasis here is on fun with a wave machine, Crazy River ride, 120 m-long slide, raging current and waterfall all to contend with. There is also a kids' pool with water 20 cm deep and water figurines and slides to keep them entertained.

For the adults there is a Wellness centre that provides salt water baths and hot whirlpools. There is also a sauna area complete with an Egyptian sauna, a wooden alpine sauna, a Turkish bath and a bio-sauna. Outside is a heated tropical garden and a large garden complete with adventure playground and volley ball nets. Aquafitness, Thai-Bo, Aerobics and Judo for children are some of the fitness opportunities offered.

Sport stadiums

Olympiastadion, Olympischer Platz 3, **T** 30 06 33. *Football matches €10. U-Bahn Olympia-Stadion (Ost), S-Bahn Olympiastadion.* Built for the 1936 Olympic Games, where Hitler so famously refused to shake Jessie Owen's hand, the stadium was partly designed by Albert Speer and is the epitome of fascist architecture: grand, neoclassic with lots of well-built naked statues. Now the stadium hosts Hertha BSC football matches, the German cup final and pop concerts. Check the local press for details.

Velodrom, Paul-Heyse-Str. 26, **T** 44 30 45, www.velodrom.de *S-Bahn Landsberger Allee. Map 2, F12, p247* A sports, athletics and pop venue that has a large swimming pool in the summer.

Goethe in the gardens
This statue of the German writer graces the edge of the Tiergarten on Ebertstrasse.

Swimming

Schwimm- und Sprunghalle im Europark, Paul-Heyse-Str. 26, **T** 42 18 63 01. *Mon-Thu 0630-2200, Fri 0900-2200, Sat 1300-1900, Sun 1000-1800. €3, €2 concessions. S-Bahn Landsberger Allee. Map 2, F12, p247* An enormous complex which also hosts international swimming competitions.

Strandbad Wannsee, Wannseebadweg, Nikolassee, **T** 80 35 612, www.bbb.berlin.de *S-Bahn Nikolassee.* A wonderful place to spend baking hot days. Make sure you get there early. It is Europe's largest inland beach with slides, sunbeds and snacks available.

Tennis

LTTC Rot-Weiss, Gottfried-von-Cramm-Weg 47-55, **T** 89 57 55 20. *S-Bahn Grunewald.* This tennis club hosts the German Womens' Open each May.

tsf, Richard-Tauber-Damm 36, **T** 74 21 091. *Daily 0700-2300. Prices for tennis and squash range between €5 and €24 per hour. U-Bahn Alt-Mariendorf.* A very comprehensive sports complex which has nine indoor tennis courts as well as squash courts, sauna and massage facilities. There is also a restaurant on the premises.

Turkish Bath

Hamam Turkish Bath, Schoko-Fabrik, Naunynstr. 72, **T** 61 51 464. *Tue-Sun 1200-2200, Sep-Jun Mon 1500-2200. U-Bahn Kottbusser Tor. Map 3, E6, p248* A typical Turkish bath where women (it is women only but boys up to 16 are permitted) relax in the stone alcoves of the baths of different temperature. Massages are also available but cost extra and sipping Turkish apple tea is a great way to finish off an extremely relaxing afternoon.

Berlin has welcomed the gay scene since the roaring 20s when Marlene Dietrich and Christopher Isherwood lived and entertained around Nollendorfplatz. Hitler's rise to power in 1933 and his deportation of gay people to the camps put a stop to this (outside Nollendorfplatz U-Bahn station there is a plaque to commemorate the victims).

However, now with an openly gay mayor of Berlin, the gay and lesbian scene is more vibrant than ever. Some areas are more gay than others, but around the centre it's all quite mixed with lots of bars and clubs being neither one nor the other, but hosting some gay nights each week. Be more careful as you go further east as you may experience more of a right-wing element. Kreuzberg has a very liberal feel to it, whereas Nollendorfplatz is more of a male scene. Friedrichshain and Prenzlauerberg are the younger brother and sister on the scene and as a result have quite an experimental feel to them.

If it's the gay scene you're looking for then you have definitely come to the right place.

Gay and Lesbian publications include *Siegessäule*, a free listings magazine, which you can find in most cafés, bars, shops and museums. It will give details of events, parties and burning issues. *Sergej* is another free listings magazine that is available almost everywhere but is a bit more glossy.

Cafés and bars

Anderes Ufer (Other Shore), Hauptstr. 157, **T** 78 41 578. *U-Bahn Kleistpark. Mon-Fri 0900-0200. Map 4, H7, p251* During the day a café with a relaxed newspaper-reading clientele. At night it has a more gay bar cool and classic feel.

Begine Café Bistro Bar, Potsdamerstr. 139. *U-Bahn Bülowstr. Daily except Sun 1700-0100. Map 4, G8, p251* A long-established women's café/bar which has a friendly atmosphere and serves very good meals. Parties, concerts and talks are also held here.

Bierhimmel , Oranienstr. 183, **T** 615 31 22. *U-Bahn Kottbusser Tor. Daily from 1400. Map 3, E4, p248* This café is quieter than the usual ones on this popular street, but with a selection of beers, cakes and coffees it is always busy. In the back room there is a cocktail bar with romantic lighting and intimate booths.

Café Berio, Massenstr. 7, **T** 216 19 46, www.berio.de *U-Bahn Nollendorfplatz. Daily 0800-0100. Map 4, G7, p251* Coffee and cake extravaganza in the gay area of Nollendorfplatz. See also p158.

Café Melitta Sundström, Mehringdamm 61, **T** 69 24 414. *U-Bahn Mehringdamm. Daily from 1000. Map 3, G1, p248* More of a student hang-out during the day but at night it turns into a hip and pumping gay bar.

Darkroom, Rodenbergstr. 23, **T** 44 49 321. *U-Bahn Schönhauser Allee. Daily 2200 -0500. Map 2, A8, p247* A rather harder crowd is drawn to Darkroom where there is indeed a dark room not to mention Naked Sex Parties every Friday and the Golden Shower Party every Saturday.

Roses, Oranienstr. 187, **T** 61 56 570. *U-Bahn Kottbusser Tor, U-Bahn Görlitzer Bahnhof. Daily 2100-0600. Map 3, E4, p248* Religious kitsch and gay service in this tiny bar decorated in deep Catholic ritual red. See also p170.

Clubs

Die 2, Wasserturm, Spandauer Damm 168, **T** 30 25 260. *Bus 145. Wed, Thu from 1900, Fri, Sat from 2200. Map 5, E2, p252* Classic tunes are played while ladies only relax in the peaceful setting of the water tower garden. At the weekends the theme is more disco.

KitKatClub, Bessemerstr. 2-14, www.kitkatclub.de *S-Bahn Papestr., U-Bahn Alt-Templehof. First Mon of each month from 2100. €5-10.* The infamous KitKatClub with rumours of dark rooms and a no-clothes door policy hosts gay nights on the first Monday of each month. Very decadent and no place for the faint-hearted. Saturday nights are popular with the gay scene.

GMF (pronounced gay m f), Schillingstr./Karl-Marx-Allee, www.wmfclub.de *U-Bahn Schillingstr. Sun from 2200. €5-10. Map 2, H9, p247* Part of the electronic dance scene, the club also has a trendy cocktail lounge which makes for a sociable and friendly atmosphere.

Schoko-Dance-Night, Mariannenstr. 6, **T** 61 51 561. *U-Bahn Kottbusser Tor. Second Sat of each month from 2100. €4. Map 3, F6, p248* A women-only night each month.

SchwuZ, Mehringdamm 61, **T** 69 37 035, www.schwuz.de *U-Bahn Mehringdamm. Fri, Sat from 2300. €6. Map 3, G1, p248* This is Berlin's oldest gay club and still packs the punters in. Themed club nights are popular, but apart from that, house, rock and techno are played on the three dance floors. Every second Friday is a mixed gay and lesbian night.

SO36, Oranienstr. 190, **T** 61 40 13 06, www.so36.de *U-Bahn Kottbusser Tor. Mon, Wed from 2200. €5. Map 3, F5, p248* A mixed night that caters to lovers of electric ballroom and hard techno. The last Saturday of each month is gay oriental night, which makes for some fantastic entertainment. Every third Saturday is a lesbian night.

Museums

Schwules Museum (Museum of Homosexuality), Mehringdamm 61, **T** 69 31 172, www.schwulesmuseum.de *U-Bahn Mehring-damm. Mon, Wed-Sun 1400-1800. €4, concessions €2. Map 4, H12, p251* The first and only of its kind this gay museum was built in 1985. There is a museum with temporary exhibitions of paintings, sketches, audio and visual installations and sculptures. The library has a collection of books and videos which are available to borrow. See also p103.

Sleeping

E Café-Pension Amsterdam, Gleimstr. 24, **T** 448 07 92, www.pension-amsterdam.de *S-Bahn and U-Bahn Schönhauser Allee. Sun-Thu 0900-0300, Fri, Sat 0900-0500. Map 2, B6/B7, p246-247* A B&B where the spacious rooms, each with bathroom and television, are good value for money. There is also a café, which is great for breakfast or brunch and at night is a busy bar that has a host of spirit nights, for example Caipirinhas at €3.50 are served on Thursdays.

D Eastside gayllery & guesthouse, Schönhauser Allee 41, **T** 43 73 54 84, www.eastside-gayllery.de *U-Bahn Eberswalder Str. Map 2, C8, p247* A quiet B&B in the centre of Prenzlauerberg. Very well situated for most bars or clubs. The rooms are spacious and each is equipped with TV and video. There is also an art shop selling postcards and posters.

D Tom's House, Eisenacherstr. 10, **T** 21 85 544. *U-Bahn Nollendorfplatz. Map 4, H6, p250* Very well situated in the heart of gay Schöneberg. Seven double bedrooms and one single. A very good-value and good-quality brunch each morning 1000-1300.

Children are very well accommodated in this city. There is a wide range of entertainment such as city farms, children's theatre, play groups, sports for kids, and museums catering to the little ones.

Berlin also has the geographical advantage of having many small parks as well as large ones like the Tiergarten. Not too far outside Berlin you will find green, forested areas like Grunewald and Wannsee which go down well with the nippers.

Being German, Berlin is amply catered for in terms of public transport and the logistics of getting a buggy on and off trams and tubes is far easier than in the UK. There are also lifts in nearly all stations so you don't have to schlep up and down stairs.

Babysitting

Aufgepasst, Berlinerstr. 50-52, Charlottenburg, **T** 85 13 723. *U-Bahn Blissestr. Mon-Fri 0900-1700. Map 4, H2, p250* Children from one year old are looked after in a private household. There is also a German–English Kindergarten for three-to-seven year olds.

Farm

Kinderbauernhof "auf dem Görlitzer Park", Wienerstr. 59b, Kreuzberg, **T** 61 17 424. *U-Bahn Görlitzer Bahnhof. Summer Mon, Tue, Thu, Fri 1000-1900, Sat, Sun 1100-1800. Winter Mon, Tue, Thu, Fri 1000-1700, Sat, Sun 1100-1700. Free. Map 3, F7, p249* A children's farm with ducks, geese, donkeys, goats and pigs.

Museums

Berliner Gruselkabinett, Schöneberger str. 23a, Kreuzberg, **T** 26 55 55 46. *S-Bahn Anhalter Bahnhof. Sun-Tue, Thu 1000-1900, Fri 1000-2000, Sat 1200-2000. Over-nines only. Adults €6.50, kids €5. Map 6, E6, p253* This museum has everything horrible that a child wants: mummies, monsters and mutations. Great fun.

Labyrinth-Kindermuseum Berlin, Osloerstr. 12, Mitte, **T** 49 30 89 01. *U-Bahn Osloer Str. Mon 0900-1300, Fri 0900-1300, 1400-1600, Sat 1300-1800, Sun 1100-1800. Adults €5, kids €3.50. Map 2, A2, p246* Children will be amused for hours. Exhibitions change.

Playtime

Abenteuerspielplatz Spirale, Westfälischestr. 16a (entrance on Münsterschestr.), Charlottenburg, **T** 86 16 068. *U-Bahn Konstanzer Str.* Pottery and handicrafts at this adventure playground for children above seven. There is also a football pitch.

Zoologischer Garten, Hardenbergplatz 8, Budapesterstr. 32, Tiergarten, **T** 25 40 10, www.zoo-berlin.de *S-Bahn and U-Bahn Zoologischer Garten. Summer daily 0900-1830, winter daily 0900-1700. Zoo or/and aquarium, adults €8/€13, kids €4/€6.50. Map 4, D4, p250* Germany's oldest zoo, dating back to 1841, is one of the world's largest and most important. It has more endangered species than almost any other zoo in Europe. There are regular events designed for kids so check the website for details.

Theatre

Berliner Figuren Theater, Yorckstr. 59, Kreuzberg, **T** 78 69 815. *S-Bahn and U-Bahn Yorckstr. Performances Mon-Fri 1000, Sun 1600. €5. Map 4, H9, p251* A puppet theatre recommended for those between three and six.

Puppentheater Berlin, Haubachstr. 26, Charlottenburg, **T** 34 21 950. *U-Bahn Richard-Wagner-Platz. Mon-Fri from 0930, Sat from 1600, Sun from 1100. Adults €5.50, kids €4. Map 5, F4, p252* A puppet theatre complete with marionettes and shadow figures. The puppeteer, Ulrich Treu, and his wife Hella have been writing, directing and performing these plays since 1996.

Puppentheater Firlefanz, Sophienstr. 10, Mitte, **T** 28 14 200. *U-Bahn Weinmeisterstr., S-Bahn Hackescher Markt. See programme for performance details. Map 7, B8, p255* This tiny but lovely puppet theatre uses old-fashioned marionettes to act out predominantly Mozart stories with the original score. For all ages.

Zaubertheater Igor Jedlin, Roscherstr. 7, Charlottenburg, **T** 32 33 777. *U-Bahn Adenauerplatz. Performances Thu-Sun 1530, Thu-Sat 2000 (entrance 1 hour before). Adults (matinée), €12, (evenings), €19, kids up to 11, €7.* This is the only magic theatre in Europe and the founder Igor Jedlin performs himself.

Directory

Airline offices

Air Berlin, **T** 0180 17 37 800. **British Airways**, Budapesterstr. 18b, **T** 0180 52 66 522. **buzz/Ryanair**, Schönefeld Airport, **T** 0180 31 02 040, www.buzz.de/www.ryanair.com **Germania**, **T** 0180 51 07 207, www.Germania-flug.de **Germanwings**, **T** 0180 59 55 855, www.germanwings.com **Lufthansa**, Kurfürstendamm 2, **T** 887 53 80. **KLM** do not have an office in town, only at Tegel airport, **T** 41 01 38 44, www.klm.de See also box, p23.

Banks and ATMs

Banks at the three airports and at Zoo Station are open for long hours and offer reasonable exchange rates. There is, however, always a minimum fee, so it is not advisable to change small amounts. The larger banks along the Kurfürstendamm in the west and along Friedrichstrasse in the east also offer reasonable rates. ATMs are everywhere in Berlin; to check on this before arriving, consult **www.forium.de** where by giving the street of your hotel, it will then locate the nearest ATM.

Bicycle hire

The Friedrichstrasse Railway station is the major centre for this, with the office situated beside the long-distance railway ticket office, **T** 20 45 45 00, www.fahrradstation.de The cost is around €12 for one day, €24 for three days and €45 for a week. Open Mon-Fri 0900-2000, Sat and Sun 1000-1600.

Car hire

This is normally cheaper if arranged in advance, but given the size of Berlin, it should be possible to arrange a car at short notice if necessary. Reckon on €100 a day all-in for car hire or €400 for a week. The following companies can arrange delivery at the three airports and also at hotels in the town: **Avis**, **T** 0180 55 577, www.avis.com **Europcar**, **T** 634 91 60, www.europcar.com **Sixt**, **T** 0180 52 52 525, www.e-sixt.de

Credit card lines
American Express, **T** 069 97 97 10 00. For reporting stolen cards.
Visa, **T** 069 79 33 19 10. Also for reporting stolen cards.

Dentists
To find out details of the nearest dentist, there is a 24-hour phone line: **T** 89 00 43 33.

Disabled
All S-Bahn and U-Bahn stations have lifts to the platforms and many buses have wheelchair access. Major museums, and most minor ones too, have wheelchair access and adapted toilets.
The **Berliner Behindertenverband** (Berlin Association for the Disabled), **T** 20 43 847, provides advice but most individual websites for museums and hotels are helpful on this. **Social services** have a special phone number for information on wheelchair hire, **T** 34 11 797.

Doctors
For 24-hour assistance, phone **T** 31 00 31.

Electricity
Plugs are two-pin and the current is 220 volts, as elsewhere on continental Europe. British and American tourists will need to bring adaptor plugs.

Embassies/Consulates
Australia, Friedrichstr. 200, **T** 880 08 80. **Eire**, Friedrichstr. 200, **T** 22 07 20. **New Zealand**, Friedrichstr. 60, **T** 20 62 10. **South Africa**, Friedrichstr. 60, **T** 22 07 30. **UK**, Wilhelmstr. 70, **T** 20 45 70. **USA**, Neustädtische Kirchstr. 4, **T** 83 050. (The American Embassy is likely to move back to its pre-war address on the Pariser Platz during the lifetime of this book.)

Emergency numbers

The ambulance (Ambulanz) and fire service (Feuerwehr) are on the same number **T** 112 and the police (Polizei) on **T** 110.

Hospitals

Hospitals are of a uniformly high standard throughout Berlin. Charges for EU nationals are very modest. The two main 24-hour hospitals are **Krankenhaus Neukölln**, Rudowerstr. 48, **T** 600 41 and **Krankenhaus Moabit**, Turmstr. 21, **T** 39 76 20 40.

Internet/email

There is a wide range of internet cafés in the immediate vicinity of Zoo Station, along Hardenbergstrasse and Joachimstalerstrasse. Others are clustered around Alexanderplatz and Hackescher Markt. Expect to pay around €3 an hour. If you stumble on one in the suburbs, and they are quite rare there, charges will be about half this. The larger hotels have business centres with computers but here charges are likely to be around €6 an hour. These are of use if other services, such as printers and photocopiers, are also needed as the all-in price covers their unlimited use.

Language schools

The **Goethe Institute** is the cultural arm of the German Government, responsible for teaching German abroad and in Germany itself. It runs language classes and also can advise on others that are properly registered. As in any capital city, this is a field which attracts more than its share of charlatans and it is important to choose wisely. The Berlin office of the institute is at Neue Schönhauserstr. 20, **T** 25 90 63, www.goethe.de

Left luggage

Left luggage lockers are available at Zoo Station and there is an office which is open 0600-2200. Tegel and Schönefeld airports also have left luggage facilities open for these hours. As many people leave on evening flights, hotels are quite happy to keep baggage in their locker rooms after clients have checked out of their rooms. Bags can also be left in the cloakroom at the Charlottenburg Palace and at other museums too if this is more convenient than returning to the hotel. It is free of charge.

Libraries
The **Berliner Stadtbibliothek** (Berlin Town Library), Breitestr. 32-36, **T** 90 22 60, www.zlb.de Open Mon-Fri 1000-1900, Sat 1000-1800 is a goldmine for any research on the city. It has nearly every book published on it, together with specialist sections dealing with each of the boroughs and specific themes. It has combined the formerly divided collections in the West and East and also stocks a wide range of magazines. There is no U-Bahn within easy walking distance but the No 100 and No 200 buses along Unter den Linden stop about 300 yards away.

Lost property
The main **Fundbüro** (Lost Property Office) is near Tempelhof Airport at 6 Platz der Luftbrücke, **T** 69 93 64 44. Open Mon and Tue 0800-1500, Thu 1300-1800, Fri 0800-1200. It is closed on Wed, Sat and Sun. Property left on public transport goes to various depots so phone **T** 25 62 30 40 which is a central number for enquiries to **BVG**, the transport authority.

Media
European editions of British and American papers are on sale on the morning of publication in and around Zoo Station and at Tegel Airport. Kiosks at Friedrichstrasse and Alexanderplatz S-Bahn stations also have a selection of English-language papers. Visitors who read German should buy the *Berliner Morgenpost* which has an extensive daily section on the city as well as coverage of national and international news. Tip and Zitty are listings magazines for young people which appear fortnightly. They also

Retail therapy
Stylish shopping on Friedrichstrasse.

have critical articles on contemporary political topics. The language is, however, very colloquial so they are often difficult for foreigners to understand. *Ex-Berliner* is a free listings magazine in English and it can be read in advance online at www.xberliner.com Only minimal German is needed for *Berlin Programm*, a monthly which gives full exhibition, concert and theatre programmes as well as museum opening hours and admission charges.

Pharmacies (late night)
Phone **T** 192 42 for details of duty chemists open at night.

Police

The Police are in the same building as the general lost property headquarters at Platz der Luftbrucke 6, **T** 69 93 79 99.

Post offices

The **Postamt** (central post office) is at Joachimstalerstr. 7 beside Zoo Station. Open 0800-2400 daily except for Sun when it opens at 1000. Another large one is at Friedrichstrasse Station. Open Mon-Fri 0600-2200, Sat-Sun 0800-2200. There are post offices at Tegel and Schönefeld Airports. Open Mon-Fri 0900-1800 and Sat 0900-1300.

Public holidays

Expect to find everything shut on Christmas Day, New Year's Day, 1 May and 3 October, Der Tag der Einheit (Unity Day) which is the new holiday commemorating reunification on 3 October 1990. Offices will often take a day off around Easter and Whitsun. 24 December is not formally a holiday but many people take it, as that evening is when the Christmas meal is eaten and presents opened.

Religious services

Details of all evangelical services are on www.bb-evangelisch.de, of Roman Catholic services on www.erzbistum-berlin.de and at the Synagogue on Oranienburgerstrasse on www.cjudaicum.de

Taxi firms

Numbers include: **T** 194 10, **T** 21 02 02, **T** 26 10 26.

Telephone

If no prefix starting with 0 is given for a phone number, it is a Berlin one. From outside the city the number will need the prefix 030. Berlin numbers can have between five and eight digits. When dialling from abroad, the prefix is 00-49-30. Numbers beginning 0180 and 0190 are to call centres and are much more expensive than local calls. Despite the widespread use of mobile phones, there are still many public phone boxes, some of which take coins and some of which take cards that can be bought from kiosks. Costs are likely to be lower than those from mobile phones and will certainly be much cheaper than calls made from hotel bedrooms. It is not good form to phone people at home after 2100.

Time
Germany is on Central European Time so is in line with most other countries in Europe. Britain and Ireland are an hour behind; the Baltic States, Finland and Greece are an hour ahead.

Toilets
The main railway stations and higher floors in department stores always have toilets. Some smaller restaurants charge for their toilets, whether they are used by customers or non-customers.

Transport enquiries
The **BVG**, responsible for all public transport in the Berlin area, has a Kundenzentrum (Customer Service Centre) with English-speaking staff at the three airports, in the bus terminal outside Zoo Station and at Schönhauser Allee S-Bahn and U-Bahn station. It has a range of leaflets in English and also maps and sells more detailed atlases and guidebooks. Particularly recommended is its leaflet "Discovering Berlin with the S-Bahn". The office can be phoned on **T** 19 449, but the best source of information is the website www.bvg.de which can be used to work out routes across the city and has updates on all service changes.

A sprint through history

1237	Date always given for the founding of Berlin.
1307	Settlements of Berlin and Cölln join together in what is now Mitte.
1451	Hohenzollern Prussian dynasty builds its first palace in Berlin. They rule until 1918.
1539	The first Lutheran sermon is preached in Berlin.
1600	Following an outbreak of "black death" the population of Berlin drops by a third to 12,000.
1630	Berlin looted by the Swedish Army during the Thirty Years' War (1618-1648). Population drops to 6,000.
1671	50 Jewish families expelled from Vienna are allowed to settle anywhere in Berlin.
1685	About 5,000 Huguenot refugees expelled from France settle in Berlin to form 20% of the population.
1735	A city wall nine miles long is built with 14 gates, to prevent soldiers from deserting.
1756-63	During Seven Years' War, Berlin is briefly occupied by Russian and Austrian troops.
1806-08	Berlin occupied by the French under Napoleon.
1871	Berlin proclaimed capital of the new German Reich.
1877	Population reaches 1 mn. By 1905 it reaches 2 mn.
1918	Abdication of Kaiser Wilhelm II and proclamation of the Republic.
1933	Hitler appointed Chancellor. Immediate arrest of his opponents and persecution of Jewish community.
1939	Germany invades Poland, so starting the war.

1945	Berlin surrenders to Soviet forces on 2 May and is then divided into four zones of occupation between the Americans, British, French and Russians.
1949	Founding of the German Democratic Republic (East Germany) with East Berlin as its capital.
1961	The Berlin Wall is erected; West and East Berliners are banned from travelling across it.
1963	President Kennedy gives his "Ich bin ein Berliner speech", mistakenly calling himself a doughnut!
1971	Recognition of East German Government by Western powers.
1978	Austrian Chancellor Bruno Kreisky is the first Western leader to visit East Berlin.
1987	West and East organize competing celebrations for Berlin's 750th anniversary.
1989	On 9 November the East German Government opens the Berlin Wall.
1990	On 3 October West and East Berlin are brought together as Germany is reunited.
1999	German Government moves from Bonn to Berlin.
2002	The final transport link broken by the Wall is reopened – the S-Bahn between Schönhauser Allee and Jungfernheide.
	Berlin, together with most of Germany, was hit by a financial crisis. Gerhard Schröder's Government was re-elected in September, but with a smaller majority and still dependent on the Greens.

Art and architecture

15th century	Albrecht Dürer (1471-1528) is the first of many German painters to travel to Italy for inspiration.
16th century	Lucas Cranach the Elder (1472-1553), and his son Lucas Cranach the Younger (1515-1586) bring the Reformation of Martin Luther into church painting.
17th century	Andreas Schlüter (1664-1714) was the first of many architects to enjoy royal patronage and to seek inspiration from Italy, as German painters had already done.
18th century	Daniel Nikolaus Chodowiecki (1726-1801) brings realism into German art in both his portraits and his book illustrations for Goethe and Schiller. Classical Greece and Rome dominate royal taste, this trend starting with the Forum Fridericianum planned for Frederick the Great by Georg von Knobelsdorff (1699-1753) around what is now Bebelplatz, culminating in the Brandenburg Gate.
19th century	Caspar David Friedrich (1774-1840) would be the last major German painter to be influenced by religion. Before he concentrated on architecture, Karl Friedrich Schinkel (1781-1841), see p47, set a trend in what would now be called photographic landscapes and townscapes. Adolph Menzel (1815-1905) devoted his whole working life to Berlin. Schinkel takes on the mantle of von Knobelsdorff just as Berlin recovers from the short-lived occupation by the French under Napoleon. Peter Behrens (1868-1940) showed all over Berlin how factories need not be ugly. The AEG combine still proves this point. The founding of the German

Empire was marked with the building of the Reichstag, then the Berlin Cathedral and Bode Museum.

19th/20th century

From around 1870 every artistic school in Europe would be represented in Berlin. Many, such as the Secessionists, the Bauhaus or "die Brücke", would be founded there. Heinrich Zille (1858-1929) and George Grosz (1893-1959) were best known for their caricatures, Max Liebermann (1847-1935) for his portraits of anyone in Berlin society, and Käthe Kollwitz (1867-1945) for her passionate depiction of poverty in Prenzlauerberg. This was a period of experimentation and of daring, when Berlin replaced Munich and Dresden as the centre of German art. Fortunately the First World War had little effect on the diversity of work produced which continued unabated through the 1920s.

Rich Berlin starts to move from Tiergarten and Charlottenburg to the "garden-city" of Zehlendorf. Many of the best houses were designed by Hermann Muthesius from inspiration he got in Britain. In the 1920s the Bauhaus would look at architecture as a form of social engineering. For the first time, glass would become an important element in Berlin's buildings.

1933-1945

Within months of the Nazi seizure of power most of the artistic community had fled abroad or worked in secret. Emil Nolde (1867-1956) was the only painter of note to join the Nazi party, but this did not prevent his work being banned. Mies van der Rohe (1886-1969) tried to continue working for a few years after 1933 but then fled to the US. Otto Nagel (1894-1967) was lucky to survive imprisonment in a concentration camp and after the war would become the most famous artist in East Germany. In 1938 the Nazis tried to ridicule all their artistic opponents by organizing a travelling exhibition of "degenerate art" but the scheme completely back-fired as it simply enhanced the reputations of artists displayed in it. Having failed as an artist himself, Hitler could never accept success in others. Albert Speer is always remembered as "Hitler's architect", yet none of his grandiose plans to rebuild Berlin as "Germania" ever came to fruition. Even the Olympic Stadium, built for the 1936 games, had been designed much earlier. Most famous architects from the 1920s fled abroad early in the Nazi era.

1949-1990 It is easy to decry 40 years of painting in the East as "socialist realism" but in fact quite a variety of styles were practised and painters were as skilled as writers in slipping political criticism into seemingly "innocent" work. Sadly many were in the end driven into exile in West Germany. In West Berlin, both the public and the private sectors were keen to restore Berlin to its 1920s' eminence in the art world; if the spread of paintings could rival that in Paris and London, few exiled artists were willing to return on a permanent basis and it would be the 1970s before a totally new generation could successfully shock the establishment again. This they continue to do at the Hamburger Bahnhof modern art collection.

Architectural competition between West and East quickly became as strong as the political one. In the East, the stress in housing was on quantity and uniformity, in public buildings on size and space. Some ideas were taken directly from the USSR, such as the Television Tower. Only from the 1970s could Prussian heritage be respected and therefore restored but the Soviet stamp remained on all new buildings. The West wanted to stress its international links so invited tenders from many foreign architects as well as Germans such as Mies van der Rohe who had fled from the Nazis. ICC, the Exhibition Centre, was about 20 years ahead of its time in integrating public transport and car parking with the site. The Kulturforum was equally novel in bringing music, painting and applied art all together on one planned site.

1990-2000 To begin with, the decade combined the era of Frederick the Great with the 1920s. The government wanted its buildings to befit the new capital of Europe and the private sector was equally lavish in its creations with art galleries, shops and hotels. Luckily the Reichstag and the Potsdamer Platz were completed before money became a problem. By the end of the decade, austerity, as well as the government from Bonn, had arrived in Berlin but the city still presents a vista most other capitals would envy.

Books

From the mid-1990s older Germans suddenly felt freer to write and talk openly about the Nazi era. It was no longer necessary to deny an infatuation with Hitler, the barbarity of soldiery on the Russian front or activity in concentration camps. Equally the civilian population in the war could be portrayed as undeserving victims. Those expelled from the East as their lands were handed over to Poland and the USSR have also now been given a voice. 2002 saw a wide range of books being published on these former taboo subjects. As she was dying, **Traudl Junge**, Hitler's secretary from 1942 to 1945, authorized the publication of her diaries under the title *Bis zur letzten Stunde* (Until the Last Hour).

Günter Grass, undoubtedly Germany's most famous contemporary novelist from the former West, set his latest novel *Im Krebsgang* (Following the Crab) against the background of the sinking of the *Gustloff* in January 1945. Nine thousand people were killed after it was torpedoed by the Russians. His first novel, *Die Blechtrommel* (Tin Drum), was published in the 1960s and was an instant success. The banning of his books in East Germany simply increased his fame there during the 1970s and 1980s.

Authors who were able to remain in favour in the East tended to suffer badly after reunification. One exception was **Stefan Heym**, who as a Jew fled to America and returned to East Germany after the war. He was elected to the Bundestag following reunification. **Christa Wolf** has stayed in the literary world and in her books was allowed to discuss the pain the division of Germany brought to so many families. Younger authors such as **Jana Hensel** now write about the transition problems faced by those who had a childhood in the former East and then had to adjust suddenly to adulthood in a united Germany.

Hopefully, as political interest in contemporary Germany increases in the English-speaking world, this will be matched by a greater willingness to translate current fiction.

History

Cate, C, *The Ides of August* (1978), M. Evans and Company, Inc. This remains the classic on the drama of the night of 12/13 August 1961 when East Berlin was cut off from the West and construction of the Wall began. Whether people went out that Saturday night in West or East Berlin would determine their lives forever.

Clare, G, *Berlin Days 1946-47* (1990), Pan. Clare had to flee Vienna as a Jew in 1938, leaving his parents behind to die in the Holocaust. He came to Berlin as a British Army intelligence officer in 1946 and describes that period in his book.

Garton Ash, T, *The File* (1998), Flamingo. A foreigner in whom the secret police took great interest was Timothy Garton Ash, who wrote up his experiences with them in *The File*.

Gill, A, *A Dance between Flames. Berlin between the Wars* (1995), Abacus. This combines a history of that period with lively vignettes of day-to-day life. The photography is equally original.

Macdonogh, G, *Berlin* (1997) Sinclair-Stevenson. Macdonogh takes a thematic approach, covering executions in prison as vividly as performances at the opera.

McElvoy, A, *The Saddled Cow* (1992), Faber. McElvoy, who studied in Berlin in the late 1980s and attended the press conference where the opening of the border was announced, got to know a wide cross-section of people whose lives she describes in the book. It also contains a lively account of East Germany's history from its beginning in 1949 to its end in 1989.

Richie, A, *Faust's Metropolis* (1988, 1999), HarperCollins. When Richie published in 1988, *Faust's Metropolis* immediately became the standard history of Berlin. Its clear chronological order makes it easy to consult on particular periods of history and politics.

Shirer, W, *Rise and Fall of the Third Reich* (1999), Arrow. Shirer is best known for this book but his *This is Berlin* (2001, Arrow) has extracts from his daily broadcasts and was published posthumously.

Smith, K, *Berlin, Coming in from the Cold* (1990), Hamish Hamilton. Smith writes about the fall of the Wall and its effect on individual life.

Vassiltchikov, M, *Berlin Diaries 1940-45* (1999), Pimlico. As a white Russian Vassiltchikov was able to stay in Berlin throughout the war and became associated with the conspirators involved in the July 1944 plot to kill Hitler. Her diaries were published posthumously.

Wolf, M, *Memoirs of a Spymaster* (1998), Pimlico. Wolf was East Germany's most famous intelligence chief. His book gives great insight into the day-to-day workings of the government and its obsession with security and control.

Fiction

Harris, R, *Fatherland* (1992), Hutchinson. Had the Nazis won the war, perhaps the scenario portrayed in *Fatherland* would have become reality. The novel is set in Berlin in 1964, on the assumption that Hitler would be celebrating his 75th birthday.

Architecture

Ladd, B, *Ghosts of Berlin* (1988), University of Chicago Press. Ladd shows how architecture and politics have been so closely linked in Berlin for the last 100 years. The political decision-making behind all the city's major buildings is explained.

Language

German does not use the letters "x" or "y" except in words of foreign origin such as *x-ray* or *yoga*. The situation is the same with "c" on its own as in *café* or *curry*, although "ch" is very common. German uses the umlaut on the vowels ä, ö and ü to modify the pronunciation. German has three genders, masculine, feminine and neuter. The definite and indefinite articles, as well as adjectives, all change to match the gender of the noun and also its case. Some words have different meanings with different genders. "*See*" means "lake" when masculine, but "sea" when feminine. "The" translates into German in six different ways, according to gender and case. In the nominative case, "der" is masculine, "die" is feminine and "das" is neuter and these are used below to indicate the gender of the word listed. "Die", however, covers all three genders in the nominative plural. Plurals are formed in many different ways and are as erratic as genders. Feminine nouns tend to add an "n", masculine and neuter ones usually add an "e" or an "er" and sometimes add an umlaut to the previous vowel. Other words just add the umlaut to the last vowel and many do not change at all. Only foreign words are straightforward as they just add "s", following the original English or French.

Pronunciation

Consonants are pronounced largely as in English, with four exceptions: "V" is pronounced as "f", "Z" is pronounced as "ts", "CH" is pronounced as in the Scottish word "loch", "ST" together are pronounced as "sht".

Vowels without the umlaut are pronounced as follows: "A" is pronounced like the "a" in farmer or father, "E" is pronounced like the "a" in table or the "ai" in tail, "EE" is pronounced like the "ei" in reign, "I" is pronounced like the "i" in fish, "O" is pronounced as "oh" in English, "U" is pronounced as "oo" in English.

When the three vowels "a", "o" and "u" have an umlaut, the pronunciation changes as follows: "Ä" is like the "a" in fate or "ai" in faith, "Ö" is like the "ur" in turn and "Ü" has no English equivalent but is close to the French "u" in tu.

Greetings, courtesies

Good Morning *Guten Morgen*
Good Evening *Guten Abend*
Hello/Good Day *Guten Tag*
Thank you *Danke*
Yes *Ja*
No *Nein*
How are you? *Wie geht es Ihnen?*
What is your name? *Wie heissen Sie?*
My name is *Ich heisse*
Do you speak English *Sprechen Sie Englisch?*
Please speak slowly *Bitte, langsam sprechen*
I don't speak German *Ich spreche kein Deutsch*
I do not understand *Ich verstehe nicht*
Excuse me/sorry *Entschuldigung*
Pleased to meet you *Es freut mich*
Leave me alone *Hau ab*

Questions

How? *Wie?*
When? *Wann?*
Where? *Wo?*
Why? *Warum?*
What? *Was?*

Getting around

Airport *der Flughafen*
Arrival *die Ankunft*
Departure *die Abfahrt*

Bus Station *der Omnibusbahnhof*
Bus Stop *die Haltestelle*
Railway Station *der Zugbahnhof*
Tube (US subway) *die U-Bahn*
Platform *das Gleis*
Tram *die Strassenbahn*
Ticket *die Karte*
Ticket office *der Schalter*
Day ticket *die Tageskarte*
Daily *täglich*
Left *links*
Right *rechts*
Straight Ahead *gerade aus*
How do I get to…? *Wie fahre ich nach…?*
Where can I buy tickets? *Wo kann ich Fahrkarten kaufen?*
When does the train arrive? *Wann fährt der Zug ab/Wann kommt der Zug an?*

Accommodation

Single room *das Einzelzimmer*
Double room *das Doppelzimmer*
Twin room *das Zweibettzimmer*
Bath(room) *das Bad(ezimmer)*
Blanket *die Decke*
Light-bulb *die Birne*
Pillow *das Kopfkissen*
Electric plug *der Stecker*
Sheets *die Bettücher*
Shower *die Dusche*
Window *das Fenster*
Lift (US elevator) *der Aufzug*
Air-conditioning *die Klimaanlage*
Have you got a room for two people? *Haben Sie ein Zimmer für zwei Leute?*

Shopping

To change money *Geld umtauschen*
Banknote (US bill) *der Geldschein*
Coins *die Münzen*
Cheap *billig*
Expensive *teuer*
How much does it cost? *Wie viel kostet das?*
Can I have? *Darf ich haben?*
What's this? *Was ist das?*
Bill (US check) *die Rechnung*

Telling the time

What is the time? *Wie viel Uhr ist es?*
It is two o'clock (in the afternoon) *Es ist zwei Uhr (nachmittags)*
It is half past two *Es ist halb drei*
It is five to two *Es ist fünf Minuten vor zwei*
It is five past two *Es ist fünf Minuten nach zwei*
Midday/Midnight *Mittag/Mitternacht*
Every hour *Jede Stunde*
Every quarter of an hour *Jede Viertelstunde*
Early *Früh*
Late *Spät*
On time *Pünktlich*
Morning *Morgen*
Afternoon *Nachmittag*
Evening *Abend*
Yesterday *Gestern*
Monday *Montag*
Tuesday *Dienstag*
Wednesday *Mittwoch*
Thursday *Donnerstag*
Friday *Freitag*
Saturday *Sonnabend*
Sunday *Sonntag*

Numbers

one	*eins*	thirteen	*dreizehn*
two	*zwei*	twenty	*zwanzig*
three	*drei*	thirty	*dreissig*
four	*vier*	forty	*vierzig*
five	*fünf*	fifty	*fünfzig*
six	*sechs*	sixty	*sechzig*
seven	*sieben*	seventy	*siebzig*
eight	*acht*	eighty	*achtzig*
nine	*neun*	ninety	*neunzig*
ten	*zehn*	hundred	*hundert*
eleven	*elf*	five hundred	*fünfhundert*
twelve	*zwölf*	one thousand	*tausend*

Food glossary

der Aal eel
die Ananas pineapple
der Apfel apple
die Auberginen aubergines
die Banana banana
das Bier beer
die Birne pear
der Blumenkohl cauliflower
die Bohnen beans
die Brombeeren blackberries
das Brot bread
die Brötchen rolls
die Champignons mushrooms
der Dorsch cod
die Eier eggs
die Ente duck
die Erbsen peas
die Erdbeeren strawberries
der Fisch fish
das Fleisch meat
die Forelle trout
die Gabel fork
die Garnelen prawns
gebraten roast
das Geflügel poultry
gegrillt grilled
gekocht boiled
die Gemüse vegetables
geräuchert smoked
das Hauptgericht main course
heiss hot
die Himbeeren raspberries

der Kaffee/der Tee coffee/tea
das Kalbfleisch veal
kalt cold
die Kartoffeln potatoes
der Kohl Cabbage
der Lachs Salmon
*das Lamm*Lamb
der Löffe spoon
das Messer knife
die Milch milk
der Nachtisch sweet
die Pampelmuse grapefruit
der Pfeffer pepper
der Pfirsich peach
der Reis rice
das Rindfleisch beef
die Saft juice
die Sahne cream
der Salat lettuce
das Salz salt
der Schinken ham
das Schweinefleisch pork
der Spargel asparagus
der Speck bacon
das Sprudelwasser fizzy water
die Suppe soup
die Tomaten tomatoes
die Trauben grapes
das Wasser water
der Wein wine
die Zitrone lemon
die Zwiebeln onions

Credits

Footprint credits
Text editor: Claire Boobbyer
Series editor: Rachel Fielding

Production: Jo Morgan, Mark Thomas,
Davina Rungasamy
In-house cartography: Sarah Sorensen,
Claire Benison, Kevin Feeney, Robert
Lunn

Proof reading: Rita Winter

Design: Mytton Williams
Maps: PCGraphics (UK) Ltd

Photography credits
Front cover: Susannah Saylor
Inside: Julius Honnor
Generic images: John Matchett
Back cover: Julius Honnor

Print
Manufactured in Italy by LegoPrint
Pulp from sustainable forests

Publishing information
Footprint Berlin
1st edition
Text and maps © Footprint Handbooks
Ltd April 2003

ISBN 1 903471 57 5
CIP DATA: a catalogue record for this
book is available from the British Library

® Footprint Handbooks and the Footprint
mark are a registered trademark of
Footprint Handbooks Ltd

Published by Footprint Handbooks
6 Riverside Court
Lower Bristol Road
Bath, BA2 3DZ, UK
T +44 (0)1225 469141
F +44 (0)1225 469461
discover@footprintbooks.com
www.footprintbooks.com

Distributed in the USA by
Publishers Group West

Complete title list

Latin America & Caribbean

Argentina
Barbados (P)
Bolivia
Brazil
Caribbean Islands
Central America & Mexico
Chile
Colombia
Costa Rica
Cuba
Cusco & the Inca Trail
Dominican Republic
Ecuador & Galápagos
Guatemala
Havana (P)
Mexico
Nicaragua
Peru
Rio de Janeiro
South American
  Handbook
Venezuela

North America

Vancouver (P)
Western Canada

Africa

Cape Town (P)
East Africa
Libya
Marrakech &
  the High Atlas
Morocco
Namibia
South Africa
Tunisia
Uganda

Middle East

Egypt
Israel
Jordan
Syria & Lebanon

Asia

Bali
Bangkok & the Beaches
Cambodia
Goa
India
Indian Himalaya
Indonesia
Laos
Malaysia
Myanmar (Burma)
Nepal
Pakistan
Rajasthan & Gujarat
Singapore
South India
Sri Lanka
Sumatra
Thailand
Tibet
Vietnam

Australasia

Australia
New Zealand
Sydney (P)
West Coast Australia

Europe

Andalucía
Barcelona
Berlin (P)
Bilbao (P)
Bologna (P)
Copenhagen (P)
Croatia
Dublin (P)
Edinburgh (P)
England
Glasgow
Ireland
London
Madrid (P)
Naples (P)
Northern Spain
Paris (P)
Reykjavik (P)
Scotland
Scotland Highlands &
  Islands
Spain
Turkey

(P) denotes pocket
Handbook

For a different view…
choose a Footprint

Over 90 Footprint travel guides
Covering more than 145 of the world's most exciting
countries and cities in Latin America, the Caribbean, Africa, Indian
sub-continent, Aulasia, North America, Southeast Asia, the
Middle East and Europe.

Discover so much more…
The finest writers. In-depth knowledge. Entertaining and accessible.
Critical restaurant and hotels reviews. Lively descriptions of all the
attractions. Get away from the crowds.

Check out...

WWW...

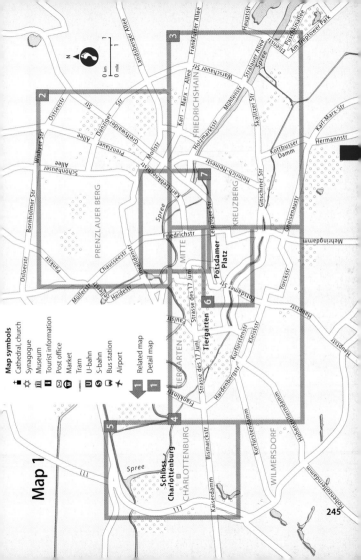

Map 1

Map symbols

✝ Cathedral, church
✡ Synagogue
🏛 Museum
ℹ Tourist information
✉ Post office
Ⓜ Market
🚊 Tram
Ⓤ U-bahn
Ⓢ S-bahn
Ⓑ Bus station
✈ Airport

1 Related map
1 Detail map

N

0 km   1
0 mile   1

Landsberger Allee
Wisbyer Str
Ostseestr
Danziger Str
Greifswalder Str
Prenzlauer Allee
Schönhauser Allee
Bornholmer Str
Osloerstr
Pankstr
Müllerstr
Chausseestr
Heidestr
Moabit
Seestr

PRENZLAUER BERG

Molistr
Karl - Liebknecht - Str
Spree
Friedrichstr
Chausseestr

MITTE

FRIEDRICHSHAIN

Frankfurter Allee
Warschauer Str
Stralauer Allee
Spree
Puschkinallee
Am Treptower Park
Eichenstr
Hauptstr

Karl - Marx - Allee
Holzmarktstr
Mühlenstr
Skalitzer Str
Kottbusser Damm
Hermannstr
Karl-Marx-Str

KREUZBERG

Heinrich-Heine-Str
Gitschiner Str
Gneisenaustr
Mehringdamm
Yorckstr
Hauptstr

6 Tiergarten
7

Strasse des 17 Juni
Potsdamer Str
Leipziger Str

Potsdamer Platz

TIERGARTEN
Strasse des 17 Juni
Paulstr
Franklinstr
Hardenbergstr
Bismarckstr
Kurfürstenstr
Kleiststr
Kurfürstendamm
Hohenzollerndamm

4
5

Spree
Schloss Charlottenburg
CHARLOTTENBURG
Kaiserdamm

WILMERSDORF

Hohenzollerndamm

2
3

1 ⬇

245

Map 2 Prenzlauerberg

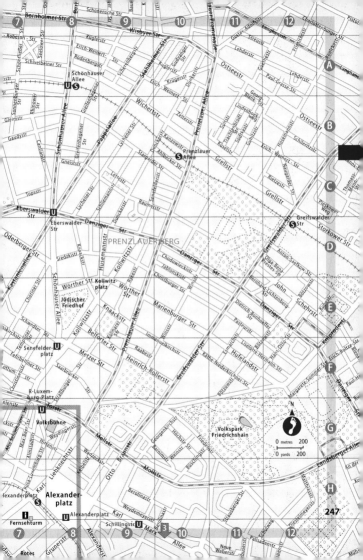

Map 3 Kreuzberg & Friedrichshain

248

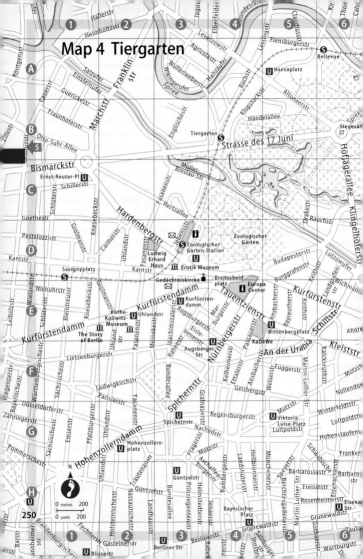

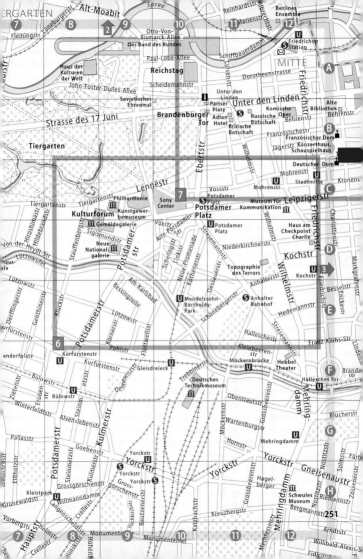

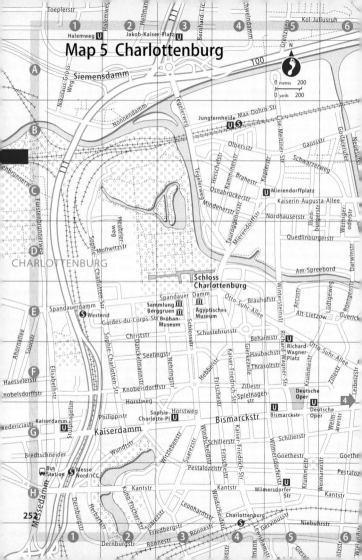

Map 5 Charlottenburg

CHARLOTTENBURG

Schloss
Charlottenburg

Sammlung
Berggruen

Ägyptisches
Museum

Bröhan-
Museum

Deutsche
Oper

Richard-
Wagner-
Platz

Bismarckstr

Kaiserdamm

Bus
Station

Messe
Nord/ICC

Westend

Halemweg

Jakob-Kaiser-Platz

Köl-Juliusruh

Siemensdamm

Toeplerstr

Halemweg

Heilmann

Bernhard-LiC

Schweidmann

Grenzweg

N

0 metres 200

0 yards 200

100

Nikolaus-Groß
Weg

Nonnendamm

Tegelerweg

Jungfernheide

Max-Dohrn-Str

Ilse-Meitner-Str

Gaussstr

Gosslerstr

Neustr

Olbersstr

Schwarzerweg

enbrunnerw

Fürstenbrunnerweg

Hertzstr

Kammingstr

Brahestr

Keplerstr

Osnabrücker
str

Mindenerstr

Mierendorffstr

Mierendorffplatz

Kaiserin-Augusta-Allee

Nordhauserstr

Ilsen-
burgerstr

Weninger-
oderstr

Darwinstr

Quedlinburgerstr

Heubner-
weg

Sophie-Mollwitzstr

Charlotten-
str

Spandauer
Damm

Otto-Suhr-
Allee

Brauhofstr

Am-Spreebord

Wintersteinstr

Arcostr

Ludtigeweg

Röntgenstr

Guerick

Alt-Lietzow

Spandauerdamm

Gardes-du-Corps-Str

Schlossstr

Schustehrusstr

Behaimstr

Richard-
Wagner-Str

Otto-Suhr-Allee

Zillestr

Einbizstr

Ahornallee

Soorstr

Christstr

Danckelmannstr

Nehringstr

Kaiser-Friedrich-Str

Gierkezeile

Haubachstr

Thrasoltstr

Krummestr

Zillestr

Elisabethstr

Seelingstr

Fritschestr

Spielhagen
str

Deutsche
Oper

Weimersdorferstr

Wilmersdorfer

Haesselerstr

nobelsdorffstr

Knobelsdorffstr

Horstweg

Sophie-
Charlotte-Pl

Sophie-Horstweg

Bismarckstr

Bismarckstr

Kaiserdamm

fredericiastr

Kaiserdamm

Stuttgarter
platz

Philippistr

Witzlebenstr

Windscheidtstr

Fritschestr

Kaiser-Friedrich-Str

Schillerstr

Schillerstr

Goethestr

Goethe

Bredtschneider

Wundstr

Suarezstr

Pestalozzistr

Weimarerstr

Pestaloz

Kantstr

Kuno-Fischer-Str

Wilmersdorfer
Str

Kantstr

Kantstr

Mecklenburg

Dernburgstr

Herbartstr

Suarezstr

Windscheidtstr

Leonhardtstr

Charlottenburg

Gervinusstr

Niebuhrstr

Dernburgstr

Röntelstr

Röntelstr

Friedbergstr

Lewishagstr

Glere

252

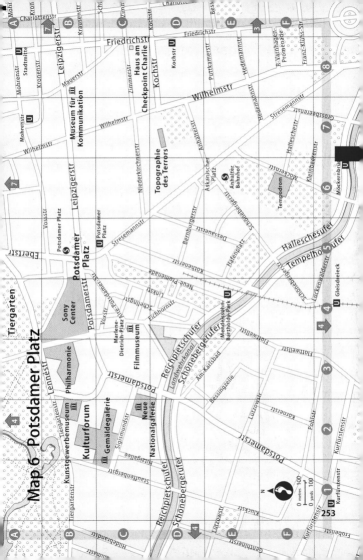

Map 6 Potsdamer Platz

Tiergarten

Charlottenstr
Charlottenstr

Friedrichstr

Haus am
Checkpoint Charlie

Museum für
Kommunikation

Topographie
des Terrors

Potsdamer
Platz

Sony
Center

Philharmonie

Kulturforum

Gemäldegalerie

Neue
Nationalgalerie

Marlene-
Dietrich-Platz

Filmmuseum

Kunstgewerbemuseum

Reichpietschufer

Schöneberger Ufer

Mendelssohn-
Bartholdy-Park

Askanischer
Platz

Anhalter
Bahnhof

Tempodrom

Gleisdieck

Hallesches Ufer

Tempelhofer Ufer

Mockernbrücke

Kreuzberg

Kochstr

Wilhelmstr

Stresemannstr

253

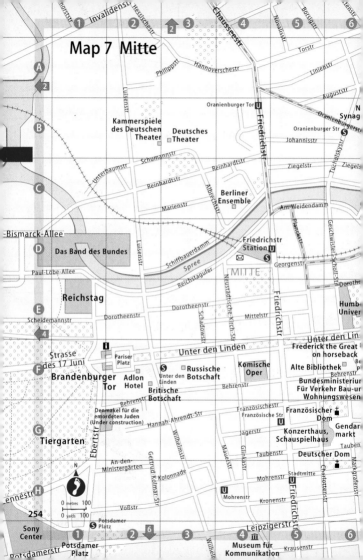

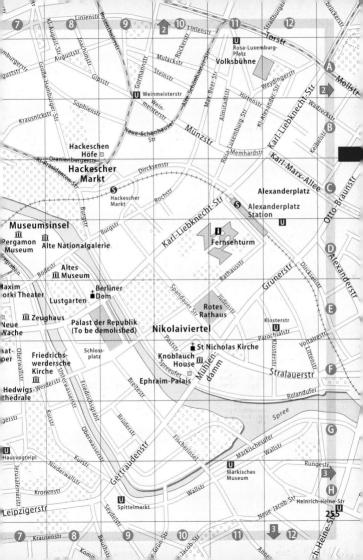

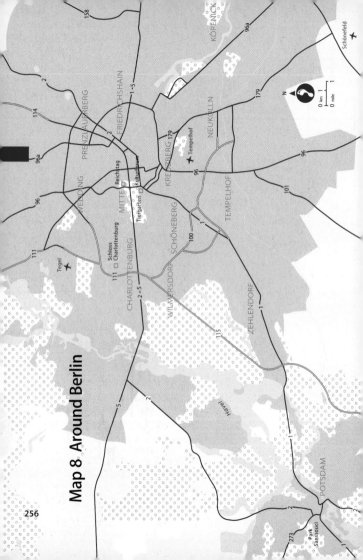

Map 8 Around Berlin